the
Second Half
of Life

the Second Half of Life

OPENING THE EIGHT
GATES OF WISDOM

Angeles Arrien

SOUNDS TRUE
Boulder, Colorado

Sounds True, Inc. Boulder, CO 80306
© 2007, 2005 by Angeles Arrien
© 2007 Foreword by John O'Donohue

First published 2005

Printed in the United States of America

ISBN 978-1-59179-572-8
Library of Congress Control Number: 2005920851

Cover photo by Penny Bauer
Cover and book design by Karen Polaski

10 9 8 7 6 5 4 3 2 1

*For all my ancestors,
and all the living elders,
for they show us
the way to wisdom*

Contents

Foreword

I t is strange to be on earth, never knowing what might happen from one moment to the next, never meeting ourselves fully, always on the way, never arriving. To be here is the greatest adventure imaginable; we are heirs to everything, and possibility beckons permanently. Yet the greatest mystery resides in the inner world of the mind. Each mind is a different shape and holds a different geography. Consequently, each of us has to inhabit his or her own soul in order to find out who he or she is and where the intimacy of his or her heart touches the world. No one else can tell you that; the maps that others have are of no use. Each life must find its true threshold, that edge where the individual gift fits the outer hunger and where the outer gift fits the inner hunger.

Experience is the arena where this whole adventure happens. The hidden structures of experience become the windows of being. This is how we unfold and enter deeper into knowing. Our times are so passionate and absorbed. It is a great era to be in the world; there are so many new horizons opening up all the time. But, as always, the greater the light is, the deeper the shadow. Rather than opening forth into growth and creativity, spirit seems to have turned in on itself and become isolated and hungry. We seem to believe that identity depends on achievement and acquisition. To be is to have. Fatally, in this pursuit, we have turned time itself into our enemy; most of us live under the despotism of stress. Everything has somehow become evicted outward. Meanwhile, inside we become lonelier and desperate. The price of outer exile begins to become apparent in the second half of life.

This is the social and spiritual context in which Dr. Arrien's book is to be evaluated. It is a wonderful contribution. Unlike most other practitioners in the contemporary spiritual field, Dr. Arrien is actually a scholar. In other words, she has the learning and skill to read our times and initiate a conversation with our tradition. Her scholarly acquaintance with the imaginative treasures of our tradition has enabled her to deliver a book that is truly luminous and penetrating. Yet this is not an abstract or merely theoretical work; it is written with a lyrical clarity, employing imagery and imagination to touch the heart as well as to invite the mind.

The assumption behind her work is that a human life can be understood in terms of a narrative of its thresholds. She identifies eight of these key frontiers. Each one is sketched in the light of the wisdom of our tradition and named in such an immediate and effective way that lends itself to easy identification. The assumption behind this is that experience does tend toward concrescence; namely, everything does not lie simply side-by-side or remain blurred forever. There are times when life sharpens, things come in to focus and, gradually, you become aware that you are standing before a threshold. There is no way back to where you were before, and there is no way out but through. Angeles Arrien is a scholar who has dedicated a lifetime's work to such frontiers and their crossings. In this book her touch is always sure, enlightening, and instructive. But the book also exhibits a generosity in that it leaves room for the reader to enter into its journey. In the evocation of each threshold, there is space specifically constructed to enable the reader to undertake that intimate work of recognition and transformation. She offers this invitation under five titles: task, challenge, gift, reflection, and practice.

This book would make a lovely companion to any human journey that is interested in creativity and the spirituality of integration and transfiguration. It is wise, even tempered, and generous. If people were to take this book up, work with it and act on its invitations, it would lead to huge cultural change. People would suddenly come into possession of their creative agency, potential, and responsibility. Citizenship would again become a wonderful cultural invitation and invigoration. In a time of anxiety and creeping despair, Dr. Angeles Arrien has offered us a necessary gift, a gift that finds the missing bridge between the inner life and the outer world. Use it deeply!!

John O'Donohue
2007

Acknowledgments

A thousand cranes bring
beauty and wisdom into form.
Asian saying

Every individual's life and any creative enterprise is influenced and shaped by many people. Such is the case for me and for this book. I am so grateful and blessed to have had the deep influence of my Basque roots and heritage, guidance from my beloved family and elders, and consistent support from my sister, Joanne. My life continues to be enriched by my close friends, colleagues, staff, and all the students and participants who have attended my classes, workshops, and seminars over the past thirty years. From all of these profound influences, I continue to be inspired to become a better person. I have been touched by the honest feedback, support, and generosity that I have had the privilege to receive from you. Forever, thank you.

This book would not exist without the talent and vision of two very competent and gifted women — Tami Simon of Sounds True and my agent Kim Witherspoon. They both supported, with unwavering commitment and trust, transferring the original information from a Sounds True tape series into book form. With the help of Michael Taft, the tapes were transcribed and synthesized into a book proposal. During the beginning phases of manuscript development, I received feedback and editorial input from Joan Oliver, Liz Pearle, and Gail Winston, which helped me clarify the specific book I wanted to write about the second half of life. Also invaluable was the quality feedback given to me about the book's context and content by my colleague, Patrick O'Neill. I am grateful to the editorial gifts and talents of Sheridan McCarthy and Stanton Nelson, who helped me manifest this book into what it is now.

The extraordinary design and beauty present throughout this book were created by Bren Frisch and Karen Polaski for Sounds True. I am appreciative to Adele Schwartz and Thea Bellos for their initial photographs of gates and portals, which clarified what was truly needed to visually support the information. I was delighted to discover Penny Bauer's images of elder hands in her photographic series "In the Hands of Wisdom," from which selected photographs were chosen to introduce each chapter. Her exquisite visual work contributes to the mystery and beauty we will encounter in the second half of life.

My outstanding staff has helped me beyond measure to bring this book into its present form. Tenzin Lhadron, my full-time executive administrator, was there with every aspect of the book's evolution. She entered the material with precision, attention, and competence. She was always available to reread, edit, and restructure as I worked through each chapter. Her clarity, enthusiasm, flexibility, and keen insight were invaluable and consistent throughout the writing process. It is not often that creativity can be met with such grace, ease, joy, and acuity, which she consistently embodied. Twainhart Hill has supported me in every book I have written by obtaining the necessary permissions.

Her work in this area is always impeccable and her attention to detail exemplary. To both of you, I have unlimited gratitude and respect for your respective skills and unique gifts. And, to my Celtic friend and colleague, John O'Donohue, I am forever grateful for his presence in the world. His integrity, humor, brilliance, compassion, and spiritual depth continues to touch not only me, but thousands of people worldwide. His forthcoming book, *To Bless the Space Between Us: A Collection of Invocations and Blessings,* along with his other work can be found at www.johnodonohue.com for a guaranteed source of inspiration, solace, and a touch of Ireland. May his work and journey be blessed and protected always.

Angeles Arrien

Sausalito, California

2007

Understanding hands.
Hands that caress like delicate green leaves.
Hands, eager hands.
Hands that gather knowledge from great books,
Braille books.
Hands that fill empty space with livable things.
Hands so quiet, folded on a book.

Hands, forgetful of the words they have read all
Night.
Hands asleep on the open page.
Strong hands that sow and reap thought.
Hands tremulous and ecstatic listening to music.
Hands keeping the rhythm of song and dance.

Anne Sullivan Macy
"Hands"

The Bushman storytellers talk about two kinds of hunger.

They say there is physical hunger, then what they call

the Great Hunger.

That is the hunger for meaning.

There is only one thing that is truly insufferable,

and that is a life without meaning.

There is nothing wrong with the search for happiness.

But there is something great—

meaning—

which transfigures all.

When you have meaning you are content,

you belong.

Sir Laurens van der Post
in the documentary *Hasten Slowly*

Introduction

There are more of us are entering the second half of our lives than at any other time in history. Our numbers are growing rapidly, and as life expectancy continues to rise, more of us will find ourselves living much longer as elders than did our parents and grandparents.

These extra years, even decades, extend the blessings of life. Yet in many ways we are not prepared to live these years fully. Our American culture has lost the capacity to acknowledge and value elders the way many other cultures around the world do. We have forgotten the rites of passage that help us learn how to become wise elders who actively participate in our communities and live deep, fulfilling lives. Unfortunately, our culture's current perspective is that the second half of life offers only decline, disease, despair, and death.

If we are to live our best second half of life, to embrace these years and flourish in them, we need to consciously shift our cultural perspective. It is time. To know that things must change, we have only to look at the shocking fact that America has the world's highest suicide rate among elders. We can no longer ignore the wisdom that is irrevocably lost to future generations when our elders are marginalized or rendered invisible. The more challenging our world, the more we need our elders with us to share the lessons they have learned, to lend us their problem-solving skills, and to enhance our lives by imparting their unique gifts.

The rites of passage from birth to fifty years of age are well defined. We may go to school, get our first job, find life partners, raise a family, develop a career, and contribute to our communities. But the skills we developed during the first half of life are not adequate, nor are they appropriate, to support us during the second half; the tasks and requirements for growth and change are completely different. From age fifty onward, we know that there will be four broad frontiers to face:

- Retirement: from what, toward what?
- The possibility of becoming a mentor, a steward, or a grandparent.
- Coping with the natural challenges of maintaining the health of an aging body.
- Mortality: losing our loved ones, and the inevitability of our own death.

Each of these frontiers will demand from us very different attitudes, disciplines, and life skills, many of which have not yet been clearly associated with increased longevity. Each frontier will challenge us to be courageous in the face of our fears. This new terrain promises to be both daunting and exciting.

Many world tales and perennial wisdoms point to eight metaphorical gates of initiation through which we must pass in order to develop fully into wise people, or elders. These gates are archetypal passageways to deepening our experience of life in our later years. They offer powerful tools to help us shift our perspective. They map a new landscape for the second half of life, grounded in multicultural traditions that honor elders.

As we explore each archetypal gate, we will encounter myths, stories, and songs from around the world that teach us to see with fresh eyes. We will reflect upon art, poetry, symbols, and metaphor to gain understanding. Learning from wise people across many disciplines — psychology, cultural anthropology, philosophy, and others — we will deepen our experience and add new dimension to our lives.

Each gate chapter opens with an image of hands and ends with an image of feet — both symbols of the process of entering and leaving the gate. Every initiation or transition has the potential to expand our love, to teach us more about giving and receiving, and to manifest more balance and creativity in our lives — all concepts that are embodied by hands and feet. They symbolize the power to love, create, move, or change. Hands are associated with giving, receiving, and serving. They teach us about reciprocity. Feet bring us to where we can be of use. They uphold us firmly and keep us in balance while our hands do the work. Hands and feet are both extremes of the body and are obedient to our instinctual desires and thoughts. Many cultures of the world purify or mark hands and feet before or after an initiation, in recognition of their capacity to bridge the profane and sacred worlds.

The lessons offered at each of the eight gates rigorously prepare us for our initiation into elderhood. The Silver Gate challenges us to invite new experiences into our lives. The White Picket Gate asks us to reflect on the roles we have played earlier in life, and to learn to assume the new role of elder. The Clay Gate urges us to care for and enjoy our bodies, even as we come to terms with their limitations. At the Black and White

Gate, we learn to deepen our relationships in more intimate and mature ways. The Rustic Gate encourages us to use our creativity to enhance our lives, contribute to our communities, and leave a lasting legacy. At the Bone Gate, we develop the courage to be authentically ourselves in the world. The Natural Gate calls us to replenish our souls in silence and in nature and to take time for reflection. When we reach the Gold Gate, we actively engage in practices of nonattachment and prepare for our passing from this world.

The second half of life is the ultimate initiation. In it, we encounter new, unexpected, unfamiliar, and unknowable moments that remind us that we are a sacred mystery made manifest. If we truly understand what is required of us at this stage, we are blessed with an enormous opportunity to develop and embody wisdom and character. We enjoy limitless possibilities to restore, renew, and heal ourselves. And because of our increased longevity, for the first time in history we also have the opportunity to create a map of spiritual maturity for future generations to use as they enter their own later years.

How can we meet the challenges and opportunities of the second half of life? How can we do it better than has been done before? Our personal and collective work at the eight gates of initiation is an essential tool that can enable us to reclaim the rites of passage into elderhood. At each gate, we will learn from cultures that regard elders as living treasures; symbols, images, and metaphor will offer direct experience of the mysteries of initiation; and the initiatory process itself will ignite, deepen, and cultivate our wisdom and insight.

The second half of life presents us with the opportunity to develop increased depth, integrity, and character — or not. The choice is always ours. If we choose to grow and achieve ever-deepening wisdom, we must be willing to do the personal work necessary to pass through the eight gates. There are rich rewards to be had for our efforts. The tasks, challenges, and gifts presented at each gate prepare us to be wise and engaged elders who provide meaningful contributions to other individuals, families, organizations, and communities.

May our journey through the eight gates of initiation liberate us from the disparaging stereotypes of aging, and light a new path for future generations. May we be the ones to reclaim and model the dignity, grace, and authentic power that true elderhood confers. This book is offered as both a guide and a resource to encourage such a transformation in our approach to aging. It provides information, reflection, and solace for those who want to further understand the mysteries of the second half of life and deepen their experience of it.

May our conscious legacies and wise stewardship make the world a better place.

Threshold Work
at the
Eight Gates

Does one really have to fret
About enlightenment?
No matter what road I travel,
I'm going home.

Shinsho

Crucibles of Meaning: Symbols, Images, and Metaphor

The second half of life requires that we come to understand what has been most significant and meaningful in our lives. To accomplish this, we can make use of symbolic crucibles that evoke our memories and spark our imaginations. A crucible is a fired-clay vessel used to contain high-temperature chemical reactions. In alchemy, the medieval science and philosophy that sought to transmute base metals into gold, the crucible was the vessel in which the transformational process occured. In spiritual alchemy, it is a symbol of the capacity to change or transform. It is a container that reveals what is authentic within it.

Each of the eight gates of initiation makes use of figurative crucibles: symbols, images, and metaphor. These vessels contain the significance and meaning that stimulate and support our physical, emotional, and spiritual transformations during the second half of life.

Symbols, images, and metaphor have the power to reach us in deep and intimate ways, often signaling what is most important to us. When something is deeply meaningful, we often use figurative or symbolic language to express it. Meaning is expressed by all cultures through music, poetry, art, and stories. Romanian physicist and philosopher Basarab Nicolescu describes how meaning is contained in symbolic language, and explores what is beyond these expressive forms of meaning.

> *What keeps me alive is found between the images, between the words, between thought, the emptiness of feeling, and in the emptiness of the body . . . there arises the fullness and significance of life . . .*

Nicolescu tells us that the symbolic languages found in images, music, and story all point to what is meaningful, and to the hidden presence that awaits us in the spacious and empty place between thought and feeling, where our spirit resides.

The language of symbol is of the felt senses of the body, of the numinous, of the spirit, and of the heart's yearnings. It transmits meaning in a way that touches us deeply, and leads us to wisdom. When we are drawn to a particular symbol, it often signals a transition we are about to undergo, announcing its arrival and preparing us for it, and directing us toward the inner work that can help us change, deepen, and grow.

In our later years, we integrate the significant stories and dreams of our lifetimes. We are drawn to the beauty and timeless comfort found in music, art, and poetry. These creative and symbolic forms of expression bring memory and imagination together to provide opportunities for reflection and to help us see what is truly meaningful in our lives.

Symbols of Transition: Thresholds and Gates

Perseverance is a great element of success.
If you only knock long enough and loud enough at the gate,
you are sure to wake up something or somebody.

Henry Wadsworth Longfellow

Throughout history, images of thresholds and gates have served as symbolic passageways into new worlds. Imprinted on the human psyche, they herald the possibility of a new life, a new experience, or a new identity. They offer an opportunity for communion between different worlds: the sacred and profane, the internal and external, the subjective and objective, the visible and invisible, the waking and dreaming.

Symbolically, there is a marked distinction between a threshold and a gate. A threshold suggests the place or moment where transformational work, learning, or integration occurs. The gate suggests the protecting and testing that must occur before we are allowed entry and permitted to do work at the threshold. Gates are often considered places of initiation or entryways into holy places, sacred grounds, or spiritually significant transitions. Deep archetypal feelings may surface when we are "at the gate."

Instinctively, we recognize that we are required to let go of what is familiar, prepare to enter, and open ourselves to the unknown. Our passage through the gate is irreversible. After we open the gate and stand upon the threshold, we must do the work of transformation.

To thresh literally means to pound cereal grain to remove the husks and separate out the seeds. Figuratively, the threshing floor is where we tread, turn, twist, or flail as we do inner work. In our later years, it is the place of the soul's own threshing, where what is no longer necessary or aligned with our essential nature is released and discarded. Throughout our passage of the second half of life, we repeatedly come to the threshing floor to deliver ourselves to our final and holy excursion, in which we approach the opening to a hidden existence and discover a second grace.

In *The Sacred and the Profane,* Mircea Eliade tells us, "The threshold is the limit, the boundary, the frontier that distinguishes and opposes two worlds — and at the same time, is the paradoxical place where those worlds communicate, where passage from the profane to the sacred world becomes possible." In our later years, the capacity to comprehend and contain this paradox prepares us to do the threshing work required to sort through what has been most important to us during our journey.

Because we live in a society that has lost many traditional initiation rituals, we have lost the ability to recognize the signs that foreshadow transition — our modern term for initiation. We may realize that we are going through a transition, or that we are changing. But because we are unfamiliar with initiatory rites, we do not perceive that we stand at the gate. We do not comprehend that we need to open it and do the required threshing and integrative work.

But now, as we approach the eight gates of initiation into the second half of life, we have a new opportunity to learn to recognize the signs, do the threshold work required, and move forward truly changed.

Threshold into the Mystery

> . . . the actual task is to integrate the two threads of one's life
> . . . the within and the without.
> Pierre Teilhard de Chardin

Throughout our lives, transitions require that we ask for help and allow ourselves to yield to forces stronger than our wills or our egos' desires. As transitions take place during our later years, a fundamental and primal shift from ambition to meaning occurs.

This shift often takes the form of abrupt, unexpected changes in our lives—such as a surprising new interest, a career change, a significant loss, divorce, or a move to a new location—that can align us with what truly touches our hearts and has meaning for us. With this shift comes an initial restlessness, irritability, anxiety, or discontent with our current situation, and a deep questioning of the motivation surrounding our choices in career and relationships. Everything comes up for review. Previous desires and choices to attain status, power, money, fame, or strategic relationships lose meaning and become unsatisfying. Any one of these once-valued egoic needs may be radically diminished as deep congruence and authentic fulfillment emerge to be expressed.

The shift from ambition to meaning delivers us to our threshold work at the eight gates of initiation. Here we must simultaneously integrate two internal journeys. One is the archetypal vertical journey of descent and ascent in which we reclaim the authentic self and release the false self. The other journey is horizontal, twining the two threads of our internal and external experiences. These two journeys—descending and ascending, and integrating the internal and external—are essential tasks. We must undertake them if we are to develop character, acquire wisdom, and cultivate spiritual maturity.

The Journey of Descent and Ascent

> The day you were born,
> a ladder was set up to help you
> escape from this world.
> Rumi

The descent into darkness — the unknown or undeveloped aspects of our nature — and the ascent into greater awareness, authenticity, and faith lead us to a discovery of our essential selves beyond egos and personal desires. In both directions, we encounter our shadows, the unclaimed, undesired, and un-befriended aspects of our nature. To become fully developed human beings, we must confront both our demons and our angels. If we can do this successfully, we free ourselves from the illusion of who we think we are. We are delivered into the mystery of our true, essential being and are able to generate a new domain of freedom that is anchored in wisdom, love, and faith.

In his book *Transformation: Growth and Change in Adult Life,* Roger Gould explains that this freedom is hard won, especially in the experience of descent, which requires us to realistically and honestly look at our lives without denial, indulgence, or embellishment. To achieve an adult sense of freedom, we must come to terms with unresolved anger, disappointment, despair, fear, and feelings of repugnance concerning death. We can no longer harbor our illusions, aversions, or attachments. Recognizing these feelings is only the first step. We have to act, to descend into our inner terrain and dispel all that is false and at odds with our essential being. The raw experience of descent prepares the way for increased self-knowledge and self-acceptance that are honest and true, anchored in a kind of self-confidence that is neither inflated nor deflated. The descent allows us to experience the ascent with genuine hopefulness, curiosity, and an ennobled spirit. If we have done the rigorous work of descending to face our false self, we may then ascend to experience the joy of our essential self without pretense or judgment.

Throughout our lives, we witness cycles within ourselves and others as we descend and ascend. This journey carries stories of descent into betrayal, temptation, depression, and injustice: ruthless actions that derive from insecurity, pride, or the desire for revenge. It also carries the heart of all the universal stories surrounding redemption, grace, generosity, and forgiveness—ascent. A contemporary example of the journey from descent to ascent can be found in the Delancey Street Program in San Francisco created by Mimi Siebert, who has the best success rate of prisoner rehabilitation in the country. This program is committed to sustaining the personal success of former prisoners in re-entering life without becoming repeat offenders, without flirting with the journey of descent again. In our own lives, we move from descent to ascent when we face our serious mistakes and learn from them.

This journey of descent and ascent is found within all major spiritual traditions. Christian, Muslim, Jewish, Buddhist, and other faiths have specific terms to describe the journey and may refer to it as Hell (descent) or Heaven (ascent). For example, in the Old Testament story of Jacob's ladder, Jacob encounters ascending and descending angels — one of which he wrestles with for hours. In Buddhism, the Buddha ascends to the realm of the gods, where he sees that his recently deceased mother has not achieved final liberation, or nirvana. There he imparts the Abhidharma teachings on the true nature of reality and liberates his mother and all the deities trapped in the realm of cyclical existence. In the journey of descent, a Buddhist might face a myriad of sentient beings who suffer in the Hell realms, which mirror our own internal states of suffering and reflect our need to practice deep compassion.

Many traditional and indigenous societies regard the Upper World as the place to receive guidance, blessings, and ecstatic experiences, and view the Lower World as the place to which one journeys to retrieve one's lost soul and bring it back for reintegration in the Middle World — this world. The process of descending and ascending is a universal human experience, where the heavens and hells in our nature are completely revealed. In our later years, they must be integrated to aid character development and enhanced spiritual maturity.

Each of the eight gates challenges us to face both our weaknesses and strengths. As we progress through the gates, there will be times when we will descend into our own lower worlds to confront our inauthentic selves, unresolved feelings, and attachments. Each descent prepares us for the ascent, the magnificent climb that integrates more of our essential being.

Integration of the External and Internal:
Two Pathways of Meaning

Just as we must be ready to face the challenge of exploring descent and ascent during our journey through the gates, we must also come to understand two distinct kinds of meaning. One is quantitative (external and seen); the other is qualitative (internal and sensed). Both meanings give our lives significance and substance if they are equally valued, integrated, and embodied at this final threshold.

We are most familiar and most comfortable with the *quantitative*—the outer meaning of life and our outer experiences: meaningful memories, important historical events, significant opportunities, or important turning points. We may return to school, retire, get divorced or remarried, have children and grandchildren, lose friends and family to illness or death, survive accidents or trauma, excel in a field, travel, or move to a new location.

The *qualitative* life experience is often more subtle, less familiar, more internal, and representative of our soul urges—those numinous, mystical, and transpersonal experiences that occur synchronistically in spontaneous and unbidden ways. These subjective experiences often appear as inner stirrings or disturbances that provoke insight, dreams, precognitions, breakthroughs, and unexpected glimpses of the mysterious aspects of who we authentically are.

Quantitative and qualitative life experiences converge in the second half of life to be meaningfully integrated. Our nature is then rewoven into a more expansive and textured fabric. Carl Jung tells us of the dangers of over-identifying with either the outer, quantitative or inner, qualitative world rather than integrating them:

Mastery of the inner world, with a relative contempt
for the outer, must inevitably lead to great catastrophe.
Mastery of the outer world, to the exclusion of the inner,
delivers us over to the demonic forces of the latter, and
keeps us barbaric despite all outward forms of culture.

An extreme example of a delusionary "mastery of the inner world" combined with "contempt for the outer" was the mass suicide at Jonestown, in which hundreds of people followed their spiritual leader, Jim Jones, to their communal death. Over-identification with outer-world mastery to the exclusion of the inner is found in contemporary examples of corporate crime, where greedy, well-educated people are driven to misuse their talents in ruthless ways to get richer at the expense of their own ethics and integrity. In contrast, when both worlds are accessed and attended to equally, in non-extreme ways, the human spirit exemplifies unimagined courage and commitment to alleviate human suffering, restore justice, and uplift the quality of life for many. The Dalai Lama, Nelson Mandela, Rosa Parks, and Aung San Suu Kyi are all examples of individuals committed to both internal and external development. The integration of the quantitative and qualitative enables them to touch lives for the better.

Without balance in our lives, we become lopsided or incomplete. We must be vigilant in maintaining balance and access to both the inner and outer worlds. We can no longer flirt with the blind faith or lack of discernment that closes the door to outer mastery, nor can we indulge in the chronic cynicism or hopelessness that cuts us off from inner mastery. In our later years, rather than choosing one world over the other, we need to become adept at living in both.

As we progress across the thresholds of the eight gates of initiation, we will be asked to reflect on our inner and outer natures, and blend them into a stronger, more balanced experience of self.

Beyond Polarity and Duality

Wisdom looks to see the jewel or flower
shining beyond unexpected places
or secured positions.
Spanish saying

A significant shift occurs after we integrate the internal and external worlds: we move beyond polarity and duality and learn to see both worlds at once. We contain this paradox and are able to see the many options available to us. This more accepting and expansive way of thinking increases our tolerance for ambiguity, which is a function of wisdom. The ability to move beyond black or white, good or evil, helpful or harmful, signals wisdom's presence.

Although wisdom can be expressed at any age, it is less than becoming if we are not able to develop it in our later years and provide a consistent model for younger people. Our work in the second half of life demands that we neither be entrenched in the polarities of our daily experiences nor be rigid, harsh, or unforgiving in our approach. We are stretched to shift our perspective and our actions from the dualism of either/or to holding the paradox of both/and. This allows something greater and more creative to emerge. It is an essential perspective for problem solving. Wisdom always looks for the most elegant solution, the one that will create a genuine win-win and serve the greater good of the majority of people.

Two extraordinary examples of what can happen when we hold the paradox of both/and to allow something greater to emerge are the restorative justice process of South Africa's Truth and Reconciliation Commission in resolving apartheid issues and the unprecedented creativity and collaboration that created the European Union. Because the people involved avoided remaining in fixed, entrenched positions, they generated outcomes that far exceeded initial expectations or imagined results.

If we can embrace the meanings and experiences in both our internal and external worlds, melding the sacred and profane, we will be rigorously challenged to transform opposition into paradox. The essential task is to allow all sides of an issue, or pairs of opposites, to exist in equal dignity and worth until their hidden unity is revealed. This is our initiation into the embodiment of wisdom, the entry point into authentic spiritual maturation and personal transformation.

When we shift our perspective to look beyond dualities, opposites, and polarities, we can simultaneously consider many diverse options and possibilities without applying solutions that may seem quick, easy, and expedient but that are in fact premature. In our later years, it becomes imperative to increase our capacity to hold creative tension, allowing far greater and more inclusive solutions and options to emerge. By befriending and strengthening our capacity to hold paradox, we can explore the realm of deep spiritual growth. As we actualize all aspects of ourselves and weave them into an inherent symmetry and whole, we become more skillful problem solvers, mediators, stewards of justice, and models of patience and mercy. We become an unshakably wise presence that harnesses the good, true, and beautiful for the greater good of all concerned. This is wisdom's way and our primary task in the second half of life.

The Japanese poet Basho said that the greatest riddle, aside from Creation itself, was how to know the world created by the beauty of the integration of our internal and external lives. The closest he came to describing this mystery is expressed in the following poem, which he wrote in the seventeenth century:

> *Between our two lives,*
> *there is also the life of*
> *the cherry blossom.*

Basho's "life of the cherry blossom" represents the exquisite and haunting beauty of the timeless essence of our true nature, which is found at the threshold between our two lives — the internal and external worlds. Until the two are integrated, the cherry blossom symbolizes the presence of an inherent mystery that we might touch, savor, and honor, but of which we see only fleeting glimpses. In the second half of life we have the opportunity to become and radiate the life of the cherry blossom by returning home to our essential self.

the Eight Gates *of* Initiation
in the
Second Half *of* Life

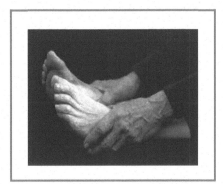

Enter by the narrow Gate.

The gate is wide that leads to perdition,

there is plenty of room on the road,

and many go that way;

but the gate that leads to life is small and the road is narrow,

and those who find it are few.

Jesus
Sermon on the Mount, Gospel of Matthew

The Power of Story

Stories are found in every culture of the world and are the oldest teaching tool we have. They are present at all rites of passage to provide a map of the tasks, challenges, tests, and gifts we may face. The Story of the Eight Gates that follows features the major universal themes I have found in world tales of aging and elderhood. I have synthesized and adapted these themes to provide the necessary context for each of the eight gates.

In going through each of the eight gates, we take an individual journey, as might a hero or heroine in an archetypal story, leaving what is familiar and embarking on a new quest. And, as is true in any universal story, we are not alone. We find many helping allies, as well as obstacles, unexpected gifts, and unforeseen circumstances that catalyze our growth and strip away what is unnecessary in our lives.

In The Story of the Eight Gates, our allies are gnomes, archetypal representations of the deep wisdom that waits to be expressed and embodied by each human being. Cross-culturally, gnomes appear in fairy tales as very wise and mischievous little people who delight in magically and practically helping people through difficult circum-stances and times of transition. In the second half of life, they are significant guides who point the way through the initiatory gates and into their mysteries.

The Story of the Eight Gates

An old gnome, wearing green boots and a rust-colored felt hat, stands at the base of an oak tree, tapping his foot on the tree's exposed root and shaking a ring of rusty old keys. With a gnarled finger, he beckons us to come closer and says with irresistible conviction:

"There are ancient mysteries to remember and never forget as you pass through eight gates in your later years. Listen closely . . .

"You came in through the Silver Gate, and you will leave through the Gold Gate. At the Silver, you are born. At the Gold, you will die. You will pass through many gates in between.

"The Silver Gate heralds the beginning of your adventure. Its reflective, shimmering surface will mesmerize you. It will urge you to leave the safety of your familiar world and approach the inner mysteries. You will be asked to summon the courage to face the unknown.

"Next, you will come to the White Picket Gate, a place of changing identities and roles. You will meet the masks you have worn previously in life and find ways to discover your true face.

"Then, you will arrive at the Clay Gate, where two old wizened gnomes stand: one will offer you a bowl of white liquid and the other a bowl of red liquid. As you pass, they will say, 'You have entered a mystery you will never understand.' The Clay Gate will teach you to foster intimacy, embrace your sensuality, and respect your body.

"The Black and White Gate is flanked by flaming torches. Their fire roars powerfully, for at this gate, love is the flame that burns everything, and only the mystery and the journey remain. You must pass through this gate with someone else. When you do, the fire will say, 'You shall both be humbled.' Here you will be asked to burn in the crucible of relationships.

"And then you will come upon the Rustic Gate, etched with distinctive designs and opened to a vast green meadow flanked by high mountains. In the middle of the meadow burns the fire that takes no wood. On a boulder near the fire sits a gnome who wags his finger and says, 'You'll never find your way out of here unless you reconnect to the creative fire.' The Rustic Gate requires that you leave behind the work of your life-dream as an offering to others.

"You will find the hidden path that takes you over the mountains to the Bone Gate. Behind the gate, ashes fall out of the sky into large vats. When you cross the threshold, you will be stripped of your false self and its remnants will be burned to cinders. The Bone Gate demands your honesty and authenticity.

"Next, you will pass through the Natural Gate and enter a deep dark wood surrounded by a beautiful desert. In the heart of that wood, an elm tree and an ash tree form an arch. It is said that all of the women in the world come from the elm tree, and all of the men come from the ash tree. This is where you will find deep contentment and satisfaction. All the happy moments of your life are found at this gate, which is flooded by natural light.

"At last, you will arrive at the Gold Gate, which is glowing and filled with a numinous light. There you will embrace your spirit and learn about surrender and release. The Gold Gate will urge you to let go and trust your own faith and indomitable spirit, as you finally pass into a mysterious invisible world filled with golden white light.

"As you travel from Silver to Gold, remember that after each gate you must reflect and practice, reflect and practice, and reflect and practice some more."

With this, the gnome snaps his fingers and disappears.

Reflection and Practice

To help you heed the gnome's reminder, I have included reflection exercises and practices at the end of each gate chapter.

Reflection is one of numerous contemplative wisdom practices found in all world traditions. In reflecting, you review, question, and reassess, gaining new insights that may provide you with choices you had not considered before, in order to learn from and integrate your experience.

Journaling is an old reflective practice, and an excellent tool for noticing what is arising in the moment. You may find it helpful to journal or make notes on the insights that come up for you in your reflections.

Spiritual traditions around the world teach that practice develops and transforms us, encourages discipline, and enables us to focus, facilitating change and increased awareness. Whenever you want to learn something new or want change to occur, you must consciously and consistently engage in a practice. Just as you learned through practice to walk, write, and speak, you can change yourself at any time through its transformative power.

Practice is meant to be active, rigorous, and dynamic. While it builds upon reflection, and allows you to see what works or does not work, it is not merely reflective, nor is it an exercise in intellectual understanding. To practice is to take daily action that supports change and provides a discipline for incorporating and strengthening new values, skills, and character qualities. Both reflection and practice are essential to cultivating and embodying wisdom in your later years.

Now it is time to begin your own journey through the eight gates of initiation in the second half of life. You have experienced many of the gates mentioned in the story during different stages of your journey; however, in your later years, opening to these eight gates of wisdom prepares you to integrate, harvest, and mend your life before your final departure into the ultimate mystery — your death and immortality.

Through the gateway of feeling your weakness lies your strength.

Through the gateway of feeling your pain lies your pleasure and joy.

Through the gateway of feeling your fear lies your security and safety.

Through the gateway of feeling your loneliness lies your capacity

to have fulfillment, love, and companionship.

Through the gateway of feeling your hopelessness

lies true and justified hope.

Through the gateway of accepting the lacks in your childhood

lies your fulfillment now.

Eva Pierrakos
The Pathwork of Self-Transformation

the Silver *gate*

Facing New Experiences
and the Unknown

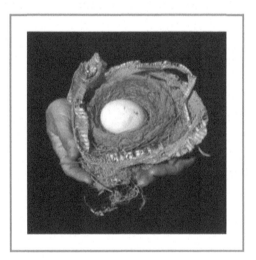

I want to praise hands
those architects that create us anew
fingers, cartographers, revealing
who we can become
and palms, cupped priestesses
worshipping the long slow curve

Ellen Bass
"To Praise"

Birth is a beginning and Death a destination;

From childhood to maturity and youth to age,

From innocence to awareness and ignorance to knowing.

From foolishness to discretion and then, perhaps to wisdom.

From weakness to strength or strength to weakness, and back again.

From health to sickness and back, we pray, to health again.

From offense to forgiveness, from loneliness to love.

From joy to gratitude, from pain to compassion.

From grief to understanding, from fear to faith.

From defeat to defeat.

Until looking backward or ahead, we see that

Victory lies not at some high place along the way,

But in having made the Journey, stage by stage.

Yom Kippur prayer

So we do not lose heart.

Though our outer nature is wasting away,

our inner nature is being renewed every day.

For this slight momentary affliction

is preparing for us an eternal weight of glory.

2 Corinthians 4:16–17

T he Silver Gate heralds the mystery of any new beginning or adventure. We have approached this gate many times over the course of our lives. Its reflective shimmering essence carries the luminous, ghostly, and mesmerizing quality of all that we have not yet experienced. Many of us arrive at this gate in the second half of life only to turn back, because we mistakenly see our elder years offering only illness, loss, depression, decline, and death. In fact, these years offer a new opportunity to reexamine the wisdom and knowledge we have gathered over time. The mysterious mirrorlike Silver Gate compels us to look past what we already know of our nature, and begin the long journey back home to our true selves.

the Task

The Silver Gate requires us to surrender our egos and begin the process of accepting the aging of the body and mind. As we choose acceptance, this gate reveals the once-hidden gifts that are now available to us, and allows us to experience new-found freedoms. If we can embrace these gifts and remain connected to sources of hope and inspiration, we can steer clear of the stereotypes of aging. We then have the opportunity to reclaim the wonder, awe, and delight that are rightfully ours in our wisdom years.

Our task at this gate is to move beyond the familiar and strengthen our capacity to develop curiosity, trust, and flexibility. Our willingness to approach the reflective Silver Gate and see ourselves anew demonstrates a desire to leave our fixed view of reality behind. At this gate, we wholeheartedly review our lives and discover what is now emerging in both our inner and outer worlds. We begin to see what truly fosters meaning and vitality for us, and what does not.

Martin Buber often spoke of what unfolds in later years and how to stay connected to that which brings surprise, hope, and inspiration. In his book *I and Thou,* he wrote, "To be old is a glorious thing when one has not unlearned what it means to begin." The desire to experience something new and unexplored, rather than regress into what is comfortable or familiar, announces the presence of the Silver Gate—the entryway to the thresholds of the second half of life. This is the initiation into all the other gates, the point at which we choose whether or not we will come fully into our wisdom years and take on the mantle of elderhood. This gate represents all that we have not yet discovered in our lives and our characters, whether it is a new belief, interest, relationship, creative project, or source of inspiration. Symbolically, it is the gate of birth; it announces conception, fosters gestation and incubation, initiates laboring, and results in the triumphant manifestation of something new. It stands alone, yet is a part of all the gates to follow.

As we age, many of us would rather stay in our "comfort zones" or habitual routines than grow or explore new experiences. But as we leave our youth and midlife and enter our later years, we need to become adventurous. We need to see our lives with new eyes so we can begin to prepare for the ultimate new experience, which is our death. The luminous Silver Gate compels us to develop these new eyes.

Theologian John O'Donohue offers a compelling approach to exploring the unknown—the practice of befriending both life and death. In his poem "Fluent," he expresses the need to explore each day anew:

> *I would love to live*
> *Like a river flows,*
> *Carried by the surprise*
> *Of its own unfolding*

Rivers are nature's teachers and exemplify flexibility, resilience, and perseverance, all resources and qualities that are both necessary and available to us in our later years. To live "Like a river flows, / Carried by the surprise / Of its own unfolding" is the supreme invitation of the second half of life, and the essential task of the Silver Gate. Here we return to a fresh innocence and resourcefulness as we fully explore the spirit of fluency, looking at our world with expanded curiosity. This gate reveals to us where we are indifferent and inflexible and where we are energized by hope, faith, and vitality.

the Challenge

The challenge of the Silver Gate is to reconnect to our regenerative forces and stay connected to them. Many cultures of the world have traditional practices to accomplish this. Indigenous people of the American Southwest believe that to cultivate wisdom and character, you must develop the capacity to be fluid and flexible like water, warm like fire, and solid like a mountain, or you will suffer soul loss. Soul loss, or disconnection from what is life-giving and meaningful, often reveals itself at the Silver Gate. Its symptoms can take the form of inertia, apathy, anxiety, emptiness, depression, futility, or numbness. It may also appear as confusion, preoccupation, self-doubt, restlessness, irritation, a tendency to be extremely critical, or a lack of vitality. These states often signal the end of something important, such as a long-term job or relationship, and the recognition that something new and regenerative has yet to emerge.

An ancient European custom, still practiced in some parts of the Spanish Pyrenees Mountains, keeps soul loss at bay. People are encouraged to celebrate their birth date each month for a year by doing something they have not done before. This practice requires discipline, ingenuity, creativity, and motivated engagement.

When we experience the new or unknown, not only do we dispel symptoms of soul loss, but we also renew our spirit, develop curiosity, reduce fear, increase creativity, and begin to befriend the final new experience, death. Whether we explore the metaphors of Southwestern native peoples, or practice welcoming something new into our lives each month, it is essential at the Silver Gate to listen deeply to what we may be longing for and to recognize restlessness or dissipation as a sign of the soul's urging us to grow and move toward something new.

Leo Tolstoy, the great Russian novelist, struggled with this dilemma in his later years. He was uncomfortable with the wide acclaim his writing had brought him. His superficial successes were unsatisfying, and he was haunted by a growing emptiness inside; he felt lost and disconnected from his soul. In his spiritual testament, *A Confession*, he wrote, "I did not know how to live." For some time, Tolstoy experienced an existential crisis as he felt caught between two lives: his successful but emotionally unfulfilling external one and his need for a meaningful and satisfying inner one. In his later years, Tolstoy gave birth to the intergrated life he longed for, and began to live a life of simplicity and contentment. He grew his own food, and lived out his days in meaningful service and meditation. His writing shifted to express what he was learning internally and what was satisfying to him — whether it was going to be published or not. What renews us often helps us realign with what has meaning for us. This realignment regenerates us, as it did Tolstoy, and helps a new aspect of ourselves to unfold — our primary task at this gate.

William Butler Yeats was another writer whose growth was propelled by something more significant and stronger than he was. He loved the sport of fencing. He felt that it rejuvenated all aspects of his nature and allowed new insights to emerge. He wrote about the meaningful impact and increased insight that fencing provided for him; it helped him get in touch with something new within.

I sometimes fence for half an hour at the day's end, and
when I close my eyes upon the pillow, I see a foil playing

before me, the button to my face. We meet always in the
deep of the mind, whatever our work, wherever our rev-
erie carries us, that other Will.

The experience of fencing created an opening for Yeats to discover "that other Will" that is always connected to what fires the soul.

The Four Fires

Universally, fire is regarded as a spiritual symbol of awakening. It is also a purifying force that can be constructive or destructive, depending on how we use it. Many sacred texts, such as the Bible, Koran, and Torah, speak of fire as a symbol of the vital life force that can be called upon for transformation, revisioning, or the transmission of renewed meaning. Traditionally, the four fires that these sacred texts refer to are *the fire of vision, the fire of the heart, the creative fire,* and *the soul's fire.* We encounter these fires throughout our lives, and during our later years we need to reconnect to them so that we can experience what truly inspires us. The fire of vision provides visions or dreams that show us possibilities and potential in our lives, inspiring us to manifest what we see or are called upon to do. The fire of the heart teaches us about what and whom we love. The creative fire signals the work that we love, a keen awareness of our gifts, and our desire to express them as a way of contributing to the world. The soul's fire calls us to be authentically who we are and serve others rather than our own egos.

Martin Luther King, Jr., Eleanor Roosevelt, Mahatma Gandhi, and Mother Teresa were seized by all four fires, as is often the case with anyone who is inspired by a great dream or who explores any one of the fires in depth. The four universal fires urge the human spirit to look deeply for meaningful connections, to manifest creativity and vision in generative ways, and to listen to the soul's promptings for deepening and renewal. Clarissa Pinkola Estés graphically describes the function and power of fire's transformative nature:

> *Deep in the wintry parts of our minds, we are hardy stock and know there is no such thing as work-free transformation. We know that we will have to burn to the ground in one way or another, and then sit right in the ashes of who we once thought we were and go on from there.*

The spirit of passionate renewal, the igniting power of fire that comes from the depths of the human spirit, is known cross-culturally by different names: as *duende* in Spain's flamenco; *verissimo* in Italian opera; *fado* in Portugal; *tango* in Argentina; *sandade* in Latin America; and *jazz* in America. All are forms of passion that hinge on the ability to hold the tension between discipline and spontaneity, to combine smoldering silence and activity, and to embody soulful expression in creative form. In *Poem of the Deep Song,* the Spanish poet Federico García Lorca wrote about the regenerative force of duende, which may be fueled by any one of the four fires, but primarily evokes the soul's fire: "The duende's arrival always means a radical change in forms. It brings to old planes unknown feelings of freshness, with the quality of something newly created, like a miracle, and it produces an almost religious enthusiasm." The Silver Gate challenges us in later years to connect with our sources of spiritual renewal. In its luminosity, it compels us to follow the internal fires and express them with duende in our external life.

the Gift

If we commit to living "Like a river flows, / Carried by the surprise / Of its own unfolding", the gift of wisdom emerges and reveals itself. Once we make this commitment in our later years, we begin to see our lives in new ways and experience many insights, epiphanies, and discoveries that renew and re-engage our curiosity. Martha McCallum, eighty-six years old, described such an experience in *What's Worth Knowing,* an anthology of interviews with individuals from seventy to ninety-plus years old.

> *One morning I was sitting at my kitchen table, staring into space. It was one of those windy days when the sun keeps coming out and going in. All of a sudden, a sunbeam crossed my kitchen table and lit up my crystal saltshaker. There were all kinds of colors and sparkles. It was one of the most beautiful sights I'd ever seen. But you know, that very same saltshaker had been on that kitchen table for over fifty years. Surely there must have been other mornings when the sun crossed the table like that, but I was just too busy getting things done. I wondered what else I'd missed. I realized this was it, this was grace.*

Recognizing grace in our lives is a blessing that comes from the curiosity, hope, flexibility, meaning, and gratitude that we regain at the Silver Gate. These gifts of renewal can flourish because they keep us connected to the spirit of duende, aligned and fed by the four fires, creating a sustainable and integrated vitality that arises from the depths of character and wisdom.

Reflections

Reflect silently on each of the following questions. The root of the word "question" is "quest," and through the process of reflection, every question becomes a quest, a journey of self-discovery. Approach the questions and sit with them; let your insights arise of their own accord, in their own time. Reflect upon these six questions and notice what is revealed to you as you approach the Silver Gate.

- Where do you experience the spirit of fluency in your life and where are you willing to live "Like a river flows, / Carried by the surprise / Of its own unfolding"?
- What generates meaning, hope, inspiration, and curiosity for you?
- Where do you experience symptoms of soul loss: inertia, apathy, emptiness, numbness, confusion, futility, discontent, anxiety?
- What private longings or callings have you repeatedly dismissed? What has prevented you from acting upon them?
- How do you renew and regenerate yourself? Where do you experience Lorca's duende?
- Reflect upon the four fires — the fire of vision, the fire of the heart, the creative fire, and the soul's fire.

What does fire reveal to you about your dreams,
work, health, relationships, creativity, and soul's
desire at this time in your life?

Practice

Tracking is an essential component of any spiritual practice or discipline. It is an active tool that develops the objective, fair-witnessing mind. In tracking, we focus attention, maintaining curiosity and equanimity as we look at whatever is surfacing in our minds in the moment. This cultivates balance, objectivity, and discernment, allowing us to see courses of action that create positive change for ourselves and others. And by tracking our experience, we can integrate it within ourselves.

As we go through life, we often see events and relationships in certain selective ways; we tend to attribute either positive or negative meanings to them. In contrast, when we track we develop the objective mind, observing without making judgments. To practice tracking in your life, become aware of your intentions, be mindful, and simply notice what is. Pay attention to where you have been, the results you are getting, and if you are "on track" as you head in a new direction.

Track the Five Stages of the Soul

A valuable approach to tracking is found in Harry R. Moody and David Carroll's book *The Five Stages of the Soul.* The five stages are *the call, the search, the struggle, the breakthrough,* and *the return.* Each is a logical extension of the preceding one, and leads naturally to the next. The stages comprise the complete cycle of our spiritual quest.

Choose an area of your life — such as work, health, finances, or relationships — that you would like to track in order to make a wise choice or decision. For example, if work is an issue, place it before you in your mind, neither denying nor indulging in your concerns. Track these concerns with curiosity and discernment as you observe what is necessary in each of the five stages of the soul:

- Where are you being called in your work? What has heart and meaning for you? What would you like to be doing? What specific actions can you take to support *the call?*

- What are you searching for in your work? What satisfies you? What contributions do you want to make? What action can you take to support *the search* for what is important for you?

- In what ways is your workplace struggling? Are you struggling within it? Do you see any patterns to this *struggle?* What can you do to disrupt these patterns and create a new dynamic?

- What breakthrough do you want to create in your work that would lead to a major advance for the organization in the next three months? What plan of action will you generate to make this *breakthrough* happen?

- The archetype of return is to come back to known experiences and to harvest a different result. What do you want to return to that you have found effective in your work? How can you apply this effectiveness to the current issue you are tracking? What would it provide for the organization and your colleagues? What action can you take to implement effective *return?*

Following the cycle of Moody and Carroll's *Five Stages of the Soul,* you can use this process to effectively track any important issue in your life. Through the practice of tracking, you will learn to align inner guidance with wise action.

Blessed be my feet that I may walk

in the path of my highest will.

Robin Morgan

the White Picket *gate*

Changing Identities,
Discovering One's True Face

We are cradled close in your hands —
And lavishly flung forth.
Rainer Maria Rilke
Book of Hours

Withdraw into yourself and look. And if you do not find yourself beautiful yet, act as does the creator of a statue that is to be made beautiful: he cuts away here, he smoothes there, he makes this line lighter, this other purer, until a lovely face has grown upon his work. So do you also: cut away all that is excessive, straighten all that is crooked, bring light to all that is overcast, labor to make all one glow of beauty and never cease chiseling your statue, until there shall shine out on you from it the godlike splendor of virtue, until you shall see the perfect goodness surely established in the stainless shrine.

Plotinus
The Enneads

In all faces

the Face of faces

is veiled as a riddle.

Nicolas of Cusa,
fifteenth-century Christian mystic

I n our later years, the White Picket Gate requires us to look at where we have become over-identified with the roles we have played or the expertise we have developed earlier in life. We begin to see clearly the ways in which we confuse our roles, skills, or professional reputations with who we actually are.

This gate reveals our changing identities and social masks. It leads us to reconsider who we think we are or are not, and rediscover the essence of who we are beyond our ambitions and our egos' needs. Each picket of this gate symbolizes a role that we have developed. We need to look at the entire span of the gate—the whole of who we have become. At this gate, we must "drop our teeth" so our face will change. The White Picket Gate is another symbol for our teeth, a metaphor for transformation and change. As we gain or lose teeth, our face changes. We first experienced this gate in childhood as we developed new teeth. We return to the White Picket Gate in our later years to embrace our new wise face as it emerges.

Thomas Browne writes of the unmasked rewards that await us at this gate in our later years: "We carry within us the wonders we seek without us." Often what we have long searched for in the external world has in fact always been within us, patiently awaiting our recognition while we took detours or busied ourselves creating identities that were unrelated to our true self.

the Task

The task at the White Picket Gate is to uncover or awaken to the essence of who we truly are beyond masks, roles, work, history, and associations. This essence holds the natural wisdom and radiance of our authentic being, reminding us that we are spiritual beings having a human experience, rather than human beings trying to have a spiritual experience. In Africa, it is believed that we have passed successfully through this wisdom gate when we have blended together our five essential faces — child, youth, adult, elder, and essence. This integration is not an easy task, as Gurdjieff warns in P. D. Ouspensky's *In Search of the Miraculous:*

> *When a man is not playing any of his usual roles, when he cannot find a suitable role in his repertoire, he feels that he is undressed. He is cold and ashamed and wants to run away from everybody. But the question arises: What does he want? A quiet life or to work on himself? If he wants a quiet life, he must certainly first of all never move out of his repertoire. In his usual roles he feels comfortable and at peace. But if he wants to work on himself, he must destroy his peace. To have them both together is in no way possible.*

This gate marks the choice to be someone who is fully alive, a courageous explorer and adventurer who is willing to disturb the comfort of familiar roles in order to discover the true face that lies beneath family conditioning and cultural imprinting.

The Integration of the Five Faces

In the second half of life, the White Picket is the gate of divestiture, where our values and identities shift from doing to being; from preparing to harvesting; from acquisition to legacy-leaving; from ambition to meaning; and from "I" to "we." Here we destroy the illusory peace provided by all our roles, uncovering our true face in order to integrate and embody the true child-youth-adult-elder-essence of our nature.

The face of the child can be retained at any age when we experience childlike wonder, awe, and curiosity. The young lad or maiden still shines through when we wear the face of the youth; we are seized with creative fire and a sense of adventure, and are comfortable in our body with our own sensuality and sexuality. The face of the adult appears at any age in one who is experienced, trustworthy, and responsible. The face of the elder, its beauty etched by time, presents a magnificence of strength, softness, and subtlety that merge to reveal a mysterious and textured wisdom; often we see this same quality of wisdom in a newborn's face. And the face of essence is the timeless, radiant face of our being's presence and essential spiritual nature.

In *Memories, Dreams, Reflections*, Carl Jung writes, "We meet ourselves time and again in a thousand disguises on the path of life." The White Picket Gate not only calls for the integration of the five faces, but compels us to awaken an inner spiritual authority, a sense of knowing the face of essence. This process always involves a shift of identity, shedding what is false in order to find our true nature. We go through witnessable changes and rebirth.

We must overcome two great obstacles to revealing the true face and integrating the five faces. We need to stop seeking the acceptance and approval of others, thereby abandoning our true nature. And we must stop performing, pretending, and hiding to sustain our false identities and cultivated masks.

Which of the five faces have we sacrificed, or been least connected to? Which ones call for integration? In what ways do social needs still persuade us to abandon ourselves? What prompts us to perform, pretend, or hide? In our later years, our goal is to notice the answers to these questions, befriend and express all five faces with equal power, and overcome the obstacles presented by the face of the ego. Our relationship to our ego identity changes significantly in the second half of life.

the Challenge

In later life at the White Picket Gate, the ego can no longer drive our experience. The face of the ego, which maintains our overdeveloped identities and masks, is required to surrender to the soul's face of essence. In his book *Shadow Dance,* David Richo creates an acronym for the ego's FACE: Fear, Attachment, Control, and Entitlement. At this gate, the ego's face is unmasked and either completely dismantled or radically diminished, as are patterns of fear, attachment, control, and entitlement (or the need to be special). All of these patterns keep us from being who we truly are. Without actively addressing the face of the ego and rigorously disrupting its patterns, we cannot grow in our wisdom years.

As we enter this gate, we must shift our allegiances from fear to curiosity, from attachment to letting go, from control to trust, and from entitlement to humility. This shift allows the ego's face to recede, the true face to emerge, the five faces to integrate, and wisdom to appear. At times, the shift can seem so awkward that we suddenly do not know who we are: we experience an identity crisis and recognize the truth of Gurdjieff's warning — if we want a quiet life, we must never move out of our repertoire of usual roles. To work on ourselves beyond these roles, we have no choice but to destroy their illusory peace.

At the White Picket Gate, we begin to see ourselves very differently as our true face emerges. This shift in self-perception creates an initial disorientation. Traditional societies often call on animals, allies, or teachers, known as shapeshifters, to glean clarity and wisdom from transitions. After my fiftieth birthday, a shift in self-perception began to occur. In a dream, many animal allies appeared to let me know that my identity was definitely changing: "And I looked into the mirror and saw squirrel ears, cat whiskers, and a pig's snout. One side was fur, the other side scales. I looked down and saw webbed feet and turtle hands, and thought to myself, *Oh my God, I'm changing.*"

To release old identities and allow the integrated face to emerge, we must become resourceful like the squirrel; flexible like the cat; practical like the pig; trusting of our intuition and ancient knowing (fur and scales); able to comfortably travel with duck's webbed feet both on land (to create) and in water (to befriend our emotions); able to fly (to explore our mind); and be at home within our inner and outer worlds (the turtle).

In her book *When the Heart Waits*, Sue Monk Kidd eloquently describes both the task and challenge of the White Picket Gate:

> *Is it possible,* I asked myself, *that I'm being summoned from some deep and holy place within? Am I being asked to enter a passage in the spiritual life — the journey from false self to true self? Am I being asked to dismantle old masks and patterns and unfold a deeper, more authentic self — the one God created me to be? Am I being compelled to disturb my inner universe in quest of the undiscovered being who clamors from within?*

In later life, we must learn to live in the formidable middle ground of our nature, where depth and character reside. We also have to notice what triggers our need to mask ourselves or flaunt our expertise in over-developed roles — and for whom we do this. We need to find the deeper or stronger identity that wants to emerge.

How can we access and know the authentic being, the face of essence, that waits to emerge fully in the second half of life? We often begin by acknowledging a deep restlessness or persistent discontent that signals the need to integrate our five faces. Then we can work to wean ourselves away from the face of the ego. These are the call, the search, and the struggle that we face at the White Picket Gate.

Perhaps the most inspiring example of someone who faced the challenge of the White Picket Gate, and thoroughly enjoyed all aspects of what it revealed, was the Spanish artist Francisco Goya. Goya once drew a picture of an old man showing all the signs of advancing years. He gave it the caption, "I'm still learning." The old man in the picture was Goya himself. Though deaf, he continued to grow in freshness and originality until his death. He saw painting as an integrative art and a portal that allowed him to discover the mysterious nature of his own being and true face.

the Gift

The White Picket Gate offers the wisdom gifts of curiosity, flexibility, and self-acceptance. When we integrate the five faces and no longer rely on the face of the ego, we release fear, attachment, control, and the need to be special from our nature. We find it uncomfortable and unnecessary to either inflate or deflate ourselves because now our self-trust and self-acceptance are fully anchored in self-sufficiency. Vestiges of arrogance and self-doubt begin disappearing at this gate. We no longer look for external acceptance and approval for self-validation. We begin to realign and experience congruence as we relax into our true face by letting go of the masks and roles that have kept both our defensive and offensive strategies in place. Embracing our wisdom face, we can meet the challenge with which the eighth-century Buddhist sage Hui-Neng is reputed to have confronted his disciples: "Show me the face you had before even your parents were born."

Reflections

Reflect upon the qualities of the five faces — the child, the youth, the adult, the elder, and the essence, the timeless radiant face of your essential nature. Can you clearly distinguish each of them and their presence in different parts of your life?

Take time to reflect back upon your life and your own five faces. Remember the qualities of the faces at each stage. The word "remember" comes from memory, the action of the mind to put the past's experiences back together. When we remember our experiences, we can integrate them.

Reflect on the following questions. You may want to journal, draw, or make a collage about the evoked memories and what is revealed to you.

- What has the face of the ego taught you? Which of its aspects are you still struggling with: fear, attachment, control, entitlement, or the need to be special?
- What faces are calling to be developed and integrated more fully: child, youth, adult, elder, essence?
- Which of these two obstacles keep you from discovering and trusting your true face: abandoning your true nature for the sake of others' acceptance and approval; or performing, pretending, and hiding because of your egoic preferences to be seen in a desired way?
- What roles, masks, or identities are difficult for you to release at this time? What illusory peace that prevents your growth do you not wish to disturb?
- What areas of your life demonstrate your current ability to embody these wisdom gifts: curiosity, flexibility, and self-acceptance?

Practice

The willingness to learn, explore, reflect, and be authentic fosters the development of wisdom. Francisco Goya used painting as a practice to develop knowledge of himself. Like Goya, consciously place yourself in a position where you are learning something new about yourself every day.

- Each day for one week, journal or make a notation regarding what you have learned about your true face that was surprising, comforting, or challenging. Wisdom is the reward for honest self-confrontation, and it is the quality that often emanates when you begin to uncover your true face.
- For one month, notice and make time to express each of your five faces: child, youth, adult, elder, and essence. Fully embrace each of these faces in some part of your daily life. Set aside time for laughter, play, and fun, which increase the wonder and awe of the child. Explore and discover some new interest or adventure, which nourishes the youth. Relish making a contribution through your work and creativity, which fosters the responsibility and trustworthiness of the adult. Steward, mentor, or alleviate suffering for others, expressing the elder's dedication and commitment to service and generativity. Dedicate time for silence and reflection, to connect with the deep being of who you are and your essence face. At

the end of the month, notice which of these faces
is the most difficult to express consistently. Use the
following month to focus on the undeveloped face.

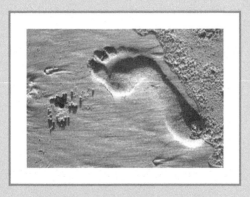

Each human soul is the footprint of God.

Meister Eckhart

the
Clay
gate

Intimacy, Sensuality,

and Sexuality

To receive everything,
one must open
one's hands and give.

Taisen Deshimaru

You and I

Have so much love,

That it

Burns like a fire,

In which we bake a lump of clay

Molded into a figure of you

And a figure of me.

Then we take both of them,

And break them into pieces,

And mix the pieces with water,

And mold again a figure of you,

And a figure of me.

I am in your clay.

You are in my clay.

In life we share a single quilt.

In death we will share one coffin.

Kuan Tao-sheng

holy flesh. . .

sacrament of intimacy; honor

the love, and passion that

brought us all

into the world.

Anonymous

T he Clay Gate is the only one that is constantly changing, never taking a solidified form. It reminds us of the
body's impermanence and daily changes. Clay is associated with the human body because of its earthly origin
and its capacity to be reshaped and transformed. As human life is
precious, so is the structure of its em-body-ment. We are as strong and
as fragile as the earth itself, and we constantly transform and reshape
ourselves. Comprised of moist fine-grained earth, clay is known for
its pliability and natural beauty. Working with it is an intimate and
sensuous experience.

The story of clay and our intimate relationship to it and to the earth
is illustrated by this ancient Roman myth:

*As Care was crossing a shallow river, she picked up
some wet clay and began to give it shape, meditating
upon what she had created. She took the clay from the
body of Earth and asked Jupiter to give it spirit. Care*

wanted to give this new being her name. But Jupiter and Earth each claimed their right to the name. Saturn, father of Jupiter, settled the dispute by saying the name would be homo *since it was made from clay, humus, or earth. At death, Earth would receive the body, and Jupiter the spirit. However, the new being would belong to Care during its lifetime, for it was she who had first shaped it.*

Like the clay with which Care worked, our concept of the body at the Clay Gate changes and shifts, and new forms emerge. At this gate in our later years, we are called upon to embrace self-care as our relationship to intimacy, sensuality, and sexuality changes.

the Task

The Clay Gate is our initiation into intimacy, sensuality, and sexuality. We are first initiated at this gate during puberty, and we continue to experience it in different ways throughout our lives.

The initiatory wisdom figures who reside behind this gate are two wizened gnomes. A male gnome holds a bowl of thick white liquid (representing the masculine mysteries), and a female gnome holds a bowl of thick red liquid (representing the feminine mysteries). The bowl of white liquid is given to every young lad who passes through this gate, and the bowl of red liquid is given to every maiden. To all of them, the gnomes say, "Now you have become initiated, and have entered a great mystery you will never understand."

The Clay Gate continually changes with our relationship to intimacy and the expression of love, passion, sensuality, and sexuality. We express our sexuality differently during every decade, as we change the ways we enjoy all our senses and appreciate beauty. In our later years, we must approach this gate differently, accepting our body's changes and challenges, supporting and caring for it, and trusting our instinctual body wisdom. Body wisdom is not found in the mind or the spirit, but in the belly—the deep core of the body, where it signals with physical sensations what feels "right" or "wrong" to us—our gut feelings.

At any age, the body can teach us to honor our limitations, trust our instincts, express our love, and sustain our health. It requires self-care, which is why in the Roman myth the body belonged to Care during its journey. It is our primary instrument for expressing our love and creativity, and making our contribution to the world. Many traditional societies believe that the body is the perfect architecture for supporting our life dreams and our journey; otherwise we would not be here. According to the Polynesians and most island peoples, the body must be respected, because it is both of the Earth and of the Mystery.

Questions arise for us to address at the Clay Gate. How can we use our common sense and trust our body wisdom? How can we walk in our inherent beauty? How can we express intimacy or sensuality as an embodiment and expression of love, or express sexuality that is in alignment with our emotional integrity? How will we rebeautify this clay, this earth of which we are made? How can we respect the miracle and beauty of the human body as it changes—the body that holds the secret of clay?

the Challenge

In later life at the Clay Gate, questions about body image, health, self-worth, stamina, and vitality surface. Our fantasy images of unending youth collide with the reality of our bodies' conditions. Maturity neither denies the body nor indulges in the illusion of youth. At the threshold of the Clay Gate, we release our attachment to our self-image and others' image of us. Accepting our changing physical reality and learning to unconditionally befriend our bodies are the major challenges at this gate. It reminds us that everything is impermanent.

Rather than face these challenges, many attempt to retrieve and sustain youthfulness in every way possible, whether through plastic surgery, multiple relationships, or marriages to much younger partners. We often see a conscious rejection of aging and avoidance of the character development that is necessary to move into the deeper task—embodying wisdom, expressing mature intimacy, exploring what is meaningful, and finally preparing for death's arrival. Accepting the aging process and trusting our body wisdom are necessary for the development of character and the expression of the authentic self.

The Clay Gate compels us to trust and care for the body. It requires that we align our sexuality and sensuality with a deep commitment to vulnerability, intimacy, and emotional integrity, so that we may fully express the love that is in our hearts. Walt Whitman touches upon love's perennial need for expression in *Leaves of Grass:*

> Youth, large lusty loving—youth, full of grace, force,
>   fascination,

Do you know that Old Age may come after you with
equal grace, force, fascination?

Sexual impulses, the need for intimacy, and our emotional desires last to the end of life, just as the need for touch, intimate words, and loving sensuous caresses remains to the last breath. In our later years, two aspects of our sensuality and sexuality need to be brought together in order for us to achieve a deeper intimacy: true acceptance and self-care of our bodies, honoring their natural functions and limitations, and shifting from the belief that we are only our bodies to the recognition that we are more than our bodies.

Intimacy, sensuality, and sexuality form a gestalt that is greater than the sum of its parts. We explore them all through the multi-dimensionality of body, mind, and spirit. The threshold at the Clay Gate lets us embody and accept all these aspects of ourselves equally, moving beyond our precon-ceived notions and cultural conditioning. This is where spirit comes fully into the body. We see the inherent beauty, which is stronger than bodily decline, in older people; we come to understand that we are looking at the radiant largesse of spirit (Heaven) as it comes through the body (Earth).

In his book *Walking Words,* South American writer Eduardo Galeano illustrates some of the diverse perspectives we have of the body, including views that the body seldom has of itself:

> *The Church says: The body is a sin.*
> *Science says: The body is a machine.*
> *Advertising says: The body is a business.*
> *The body says: I am a fiesta.*

When we recognize that our bodies are a "fiesta," we lose our self-consciousness and can embrace them fully. We can open to the deep emotional and spiritual intimacy of mature love. Margaret Fowler, editor of *Love in Bloom*, an anthology of stories about intimacy and love in later years, writes, "For older lovers, failures of the body are more acceptable than failures of the soul." Because we can begin to see each other and ourselves as more than our bodies, we can explore the deeper mysteries of who we are.

Every season of life has its own kind of love and sensual beauty, and each kind of love is fostered and deepened in an environment of intimacy. At the Clay Gate we learn that in order for intimacy to flourish, five qualities must be consistently present: honesty, trust, openness, respect, and vulnerability. In our later years, it is necessary to foster all five equally. Which of these five qualities are we most connected to and which are least developed in us? Who can ever forget our first friend, our first love, our first sexual experience, or the first tender and vulnerable moment we allowed ourselves to be truly seen by another in our physical or emotional nakedness? All of these intimate moments, and many others like them, can only expand in the presence of the five qualities. They increase our capacity to touch the spiritual and the physical aspects of ourselves simultaneously. An ancient Moorish saying inscribed on one of the walls of Spain's majestic Alhambra poignantly describes this body/soul intimacy: "When you touch the body and it reaches the soul, the bird's love song is released."

At the Clay Gate we learn to cultivate intimacy. At any age, the two greatest obstacles to intimacy are self-absorption and self-doubt. To overcome them, we must heal our self-image. In the first half of life, we often feared being hurt, so we protected ourselves and eventually may have lost our capacity to experience intimacy or fully express love. We know that we all belong to the "scar clan"; we have all been betrayed, hurt, and disappointed. We also know in our later years that it is much better to love again than to become bitter, broken, sour, or dispirited. An old Sufi saying reminds us that the greatest remorse we can experience is love unexpressed: "Oh break my heart; oh, break it again, so I can learn to love even more again." No matter what may have happened to us earlier in our lives, our work at the Clay Gate is to learn about love, trusting our body wisdom and its expression of intimacy.

the Gift

The gift that presents itself at the Clay Gate is inherent in all of us: our instinctual body wisdom. Many traditional societies believe that the body does not lie; our task is to take care of it and listen to its kinesthetic intelligence. The body flourishes or declines as we respect or disrespect it, and reveals our capacity for self-respect and respect of others.

Body wisdom teaches us our true limits and boundaries, and lets us know when we exceed what our bodies can do. In our later years, we stop abusing our bodies and honor our limits by using our energy and stamina more wisely. We learn to engage the body as a "fiesta," and celebrate and honor it for what it teaches us about ourselves.

Because the body is the instrument that allows us to express love and creativity, it lets us know when we are authentically aligned with our work and relationships, and whether or not we are willing to be intimate. When we heed the gift of body wisdom at this gate and do the work required, we expand our experience of mature intimacy by creating environments where the body will prevail and thrive in honesty, trust, openness, respect, and vulnerability.

True intimacy in later years can be expressed through a nonverbal tenderness that lets us know with certainty that all five qualities are present. Myrlie Evers, wife of civil rights leader Medgar Evers, described her experience in this way:

> *I love roses, but Medgar could never afford to buy me a florist's bouquet. So he did something better. Every year he made a ritual of giving me bare-root roses to plant in our yard, and eventually, three dozen rosebushes were the envy of our neighbors. Once in a while, Medgar would gather a bouquet, or perhaps just one rose, and hand it to me as he came through the door. It became an unspoken verse of the love between us.*

This unspoken verse of love is what the body instinctively knows and expresses in spontaneous and genuine actions, in words, and through touch. In our later years, the Clay Gate delivers us to a sweet tenderness and beauty that is fostered by the five qualities. All are available to us if we will listen to and trust our inherent body wisdom.

Reflections

Reflect upon the cycles of the earth, the seasons of nature, and your own life, decade by decade:

- When did you begin to respect your body wisdom and honor your body's functions, senses, and limitations? In what ways do you honor the wisdom of self-care? Do you do so without going to the extremes of vanity or neglect?
- What has been your relationship to intimacy, sensuality, and sexuality?
- What have you learned about your body being a "fiesta"?
- Sports, dancing, martial arts, and walking can allow you to feel more at ease with your body. When have you felt the most comfortable and free in your body?
- When did you begin to discover that you were more than your body?
- The daily experience of beauty nourishes the soul and the senses. How can you bring more beauty into your life?
- Write in your journal or create a poem honoring your most intimate moments and experiences of this last year. What has changed for you from previous years?
- Of the five qualities that are necessary to foster intimacy (honesty, trust, respect, openness, and vulnerability), which do you need to cultivate and develop at this time?

- The two greatest obstacles to intimacy, self-absorption and self-doubt, indicate that self-trust and self-image issues are still present. Which obstacles do you need to work through and diminish?

Practice

At the Clay Gate, we encounter our relationships to intimacy, trust, sensuality, acceptance, love, and beauty. We can deepen our experience of these through daily practice. When we take an action every day, we expand our capacity to move beyond the comfortable or familiar, and create new opportunities for growth and change.

- Every day, extend gratitude to your body, for it is the instrument that allows you to experience life. What do you like and appreciate about your body? Honor and care for it in special ways through rest, exercise, nutrition, and relaxation. Adorn it, perfume and massage it, decorate it comfortably using the beauty of color and texture to bring pleasure to your senses. Tending to the body increases personal positive regard and self-respect.

- For seven days, observe what gets in the way of expressing yourself in honest, trusting, open, respectful, and vulnerable ways. This is invaluable information, because it signals where your ability to consistently foster intimacy is limited. Listening to your body wisdom teaches you about intimacy. Notice daily how your body tenses or relaxes in varied circumstances and in relation to certain people, or moves toward or away from certain situations.

- For an entire season, take an action every day that brings more intimacy, beauty, sensuality, and love into your home and relationships. Each day, make a point of telling your loved ones what you genuinely appreciate about them. What did you learn from them, and where have they touched you? What are the little things you love about them? What do you appreciate about your friends and colleagues? Send them a card or flowers, invite them to lunch, or do something anonymously that you know will make them happy.

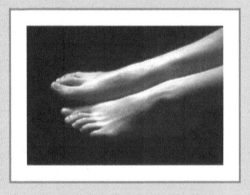

. . . the color of clay, warm with promise . . .

Robin Morgan
"The Network of the Imaginary Mother"

the
Black and White
gate

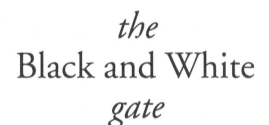

Relationships: The Crucible of Love, Generosity, Betrayal, and Forgiveness

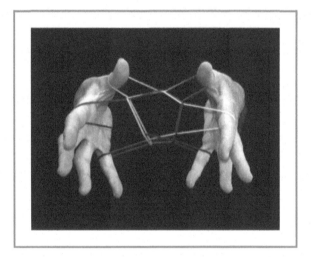

He drew a circle that shut me out —
Heretic, rebel, a thing to flout.
But Love and I had the wit to win:
We drew a circle that took him in!

Edwin Markham
"Outwitted"

May the door of this home be wide enough

to receive all who hunger for love,

all who are lonely for friendship.

May it welcome all who have cares to unburden,

thanks to express, hopes to nurture.

May the door of this house be narrow enough

to shut out pettiness and pride, envy, and enmity.

May its threshold be no stumbling block

to young or strained feet.

May it be too high to admit to complacency,

selfishness, and harshness.

May this home be for all who enter,

the doorway to richness and a more meaningful life.

The Siddur of Shir Chadash

Love is not a doctrine.

Peace is not an international agreement.

Love and Peace are beings who

live as possibilities in us.

M.C. Richards

The Black and White Gate is a double gate. One side is black with a white knob and the other side is white with a black knob. It is flanked by flaming torches, and when we open it, their fire roars to remind us that here we will be tempered and humbled.

This is the gate of relationships, the only one that we must go through in the company of at least one other person in order to learn about love and the expression of love. Here we overcome self-imposed isolation and cast out whatever cynicism has infected us or our relationships. At this gate, relationships are a mirror, reflecting who we are and who we are not beneath our cleverness and our need to be seen in the ways we prefer.

Here, all kinds of relationships are our teachers: those between mates and lovers; parents and children; colleagues and friends; teachers and students; employers and employees. At this gate, we also consider our relationships with ourselves and with our spirituality. As we go through this gate with others, we learn about loyalty, betrayal, forgiveness, generosity, and the four kinds of love available to us to express in different relationships.

Four Kinds of Love

The Western tradition identifies four kinds of love:

- eros — the drive to unify, to create, and procreate; the urge toward higher forms of being and relationship
- libido — physical desire, sexuality, sensuality, lust
- philia — friendship; brotherly or sisterly love
- agape or caritas — the compassionate heart or transfigured desire; the love devoted to the respect and welfare of others; the commitment to doing no harm

Every experience of authentic love is a blend, in varying proportions, of these four. The Dalai Lama urges us to integrate love in all the ways we can when he says, "Love and compassion are necessities, not luxuries. Without them, humanity cannot survive."

the Task

———

At the Black and White Gate, we review and reassess our conduct in the art and craft of relationships. This gate requires that we face the history of all our relationships: with ourselves, friends, colleagues, and family members, as well as with organizations, teams, and communities.

Here, we are reminded of our purpose as human beings —a miraculous species born to learn about love and to create. Any relationship can function as a conduit for both manifesting creativity and mirroring to us the extent of our ability to express love.

This gate reveals what we are learning about love in all its forms of expression, as well as what prevents us from expressing the love that is in our hearts. We begin to release our reliance on fear or pride to protect us. We recognize in our later years that the only way to come home to our spiritual nature is to express our love nature.

We need to bless those who challenge us to love more fully, for they are great teachers who show us when we are open-hearted or closed-hearted, full-hearted or half-hearted, and strong-hearted or weak-hearted in our relationships. The shadow side of the open heart is closed-heartedness, which reveals where we still hold resentments and old disappointments instead of expressing the trust, curiosity, and generosity of the open heart. Closed-heartedness tells us where we have forgiveness work to do, and where we need to mend our relationships. Half-hearted behaviors are the opposite of full-heartedness and reveal our ambivalence and lack of commitment, which create mixed messages, mistrust, and misunderstanding. When we are full-hearted, rather than half-hearted, we are clear, consistent, and trustworthy. Weak-heartedness indicates where we lack the courage to be strong-hearted with others or are unable to face conflict in honest creative ways; instead, we tend to appease others and avoid conflict. The strong heart aligns with courage and integrity and meets conflict as an invitation to creative problem-solving. At this gate, it is essential to reclaim the open, full, clear, and strong heart, and to track what or who ignites our moving into close-hearted, half-hearted, and weak-hearted behaviors.

At the Black and White Gate we explore everything we know about love. We discover what knowledge of love we want to pass on to future generations. In the second half of life we must mend our relationships, especially where we know we have harmed or betrayed others. We must let go of our grudges, disappointments, resentments, and desire for revenge. This is the gate of course correction, acceptance of loss, and attention to whatever reparations our relationships may need.

In the second half of life, this gate asks us to develop a mature heart which expresses love with wisdom. We confront and release romantic infatuation. We see it for what it is: the obsessive pursuit of an unrealistic, unsustainable ideal. We are faced with questions: In what ways do we still confuse love with infatuation? What obstacles prevent us from letting go of patterns of immature love and fully expressing mature love? When do we consciously isolate ourselves rather than engage in relationships? Who were the teachers of our hearts? What are we learning about love? What do we know about love?

the Challenge

Many spiritual traditions teach that being in any kind of significant relationship with another person is the most rigorous spiritual practice we can undertake. In relationships, we confront both what is easy and difficult to accept about our nature. Relationships teach us about our capacity for love, forgiveness, and respect for others.

At the Black and White Gate, we face both our positive and negative shadows. The positive shadow consists of our gifts and other positive aspects of ourselves that we have not claimed or fully expressed. The aspects of ourselves that we judge negatively, or are unwilling to acknowledge, comprise our negative shadow. What positive or negative aspects of ourselves are we unwilling to embrace? What positive or negative aspects of others do we desire to have, or hope we do not possess? In later years, we need to befriend both shadows. According to Carl Jung, any relationship is a crucible in which we reflect both aspects of ourselves — the light and the dark — to each other, mirroring the gifts of learning and unfolding. Jung wrote in *Memories, Dreams, Reflections,* "To confront a person with their own shadow is to show them the light." Relationships give us the opportunity to do this for each other.

The second half of life challenges us to love differently in relationships, not controlling or possessing others, and not permitting ourselves to be controlled or possessed. Marge Piercy writes about this kind of love in her poem, "To Have Without Holding":

> *Learning to love differently is hard,*
> *love with the hands wide open, love*
> *with the doors banging on their hinges,*
> *the cupboard unlocked, the wind*
> *roaring and whimpering in the rooms*
> *rustling the sheets and snapping the blinds*
> *that thwack like rubber bands*
> *in an open palm.*

This is the gate where we learn to love openly without any posturing or hidden agendas. Love that grows from emotional integrity, without restraint or defenses, supports mutual freedom and growth, and opens the doorway to mature love.

The Power of Gratitude

In his book *Essential Spirituality*, Roger Walsh describes three ways in which the world's great religions teach us how to develop mature love and a wise heart: cultivating attitudes and practices that lessen difficult emotions such as fear and anger, cultivating qualities such as gratitude and generosity that foster love, and cultivating love itself. We learn to extend love through genuine acknowledgment, appreciation, validation, and recognition.

One of the most powerful ways we express love is through gratitude; it keeps our hearts open to each other. It is impossible to have a closed heart when we are thankful. This practice keeps us learning and growing, and frees our generosity.

The practice of offering gratitude bestows many benefits. It dissolves negative feelings. Anger, arrogance, and jealousy melt in its embrace. Fear and defensiveness dissolve. Gratitude diminishes barriers to love and evokes happiness, which is itself a powerfully healing and beneficial emotion. It establishes a foundation for the challenging work of forgiveness in relationships when we have experienced betrayal, loss, broken promises, deceptions, and disappointments. Gratitude keeps alive what has meaning for us and fosters our capacity to apologize and forgive.

As gratitude grows out of love, its expression creates an opening through which increased generosity and good will can emerge. The Persian poet Rumi described the great resource of love as a fire that resides in the heart: "Love is that flame that once kindled burns everything, and only the mystery and the journey remain."

Overcoming Fear and Pride

The two greatest obstacles to love's full expression in relationships are fear and pride. The Black and White Gate offers the opportunity to overcome them.

Fear constricts energy, immobilizes us, and holds us in the status quo. Many of our fears are generated in our minds and may never manifest. They are seldom real. The two primal fears that all human beings face are the fear of loss or abandonment, and the fear of being restricted or trapped. If we fear loss, we tend to restrict others by becoming needy and controlling. If we fear being trapped, we may abandon ourselves or others. We may mistrust our ability to set appropriate limits and boundaries, and instead become rebellious or excessively independent. We may tend to do both simultaneously when we are genuinely terrified. Courage and self-trust are the antidotes to fear and unhealthy pride.

Healthy pride grows out of satisfaction in doing something well; in achieving excellence we learn from our mistakes and develop greater effectiveness. For example, athletes practice again and again, making one mistake after another as they increase their strength, agility, and flexibility. They learn what works and what doesn't, and with practice, they excel. Their healthy pride in their accomplishments arises from their commitment to discipline and action. They work to excel at a variety of skills in a sport they genuinely love.

Unhealthy or excessive pride expresses itself in arrogance, a sense of entitlement, difficulty owning mistakes, and addiction to perfection. This type of pride arises from low self-esteem, the need to be seen in a desired way, and a strong inner critic or judgmental nature. When we let go of unhealthy pride, we return to a natural, balanced state of confidence.

Fear and pride close our hearts and lead to strategies of defensiveness, offensiveness, and clever rationales. These strategic behaviors often result in anger, impatience, and intolerance, which harm others. During our later years, the Black and White Gate requires that we express more patience, tolerance, and compassion in our relationships. Our growing ability to do so signals that we are overcoming fear and pride. This, along with the practice of gratitude, prepares the ground for forgiveness work.

The Power of Forgiveness

Cultivating gratitude, generosity, and genuine wholehearted forgiveness is the transformational character work of the Black and White Gate. Forgiveness offers healing for us and others. It nurtures deep love and generosity of spirit. In our later years, we need to consciously invite forgiveness in three ways:

- forgive ourselves for participating in self-deception or abandoning ourselves to win acceptance and approval
- request forgiveness from those we have hurt, which requires us to do reparation work and make a commitment not to repeat the mistake
- forgive those who have hurt us, and demonstrate to them our willingness to let go of past hurts, resentments, disappointments, and betrayals

Forgiveness work begins when we can extend a genuine apology and perform acts of reparation, rectification, and reconciliation. True apology reduces fear and anger, dispels resentment, and creates an opening for generosity and forgiveness to emerge. It is the first step to making amends. It is an act of contrition, a way to demonstrate our regret or remorse for our part in creating misunderstanding, strain, or harm in a relationship.

There is an important distinction between regret and remorse. Regret is the recognition that we have caused an injury and that it is our responsibility to rectify it. If we do not address this responsibility, we feel guilt and shame. If we indulge in regret, it can paralyze us and prevent us from making reparation. Remorse, on the other hand, is the unshakable knowledge that we have injured someone; this grieves us, and we move immediately to acts of reparation. Through remorse, we learn from our experience and change our behavior, ensuring that we never repeat the harm that we have done. By taking action, we can release guilt and shame, and reconnect to our natural humility and integrity.

Forgiveness cannot be forced, but it can be practiced. The following forgiveness prayers by Rabbi Zalman Schachter-Shalomi in his book *From Age-ing to Sage-ing* are offered as a daily practice. They are prayers in the original meaning of the word: entreaties. They entreat us to awaken:

> *Eternal Friend, I hereby forgive anyone who hurt, up-*
> *set, or offended me; damaging my body, my property, my*
> *reputation, or people whom I love; whether done acci-*
> *dentally or willfully, carelessly or purposely; whether done*
> *with words, deeds, thoughts, or attitudes; whether in this*

lifetime or another incarnation. I forgive every person;
may no one be punished because of me.

After the forgiveness of others, the prayer continues:

Eternal Friend, help me to be thoughtful and to resist
committing acts that are evil in Your eyes. Whatever sins
I have committed, please blot them out in Your abundant
kindness and spare me suffering or harmful illnesses. May
the words of my mouth and the meditations of my heart
find acceptance before You, Eternal Friend, who protects
and frees me.

Forgiveness and reparation are both the primary challenge and the ultimate task at the Black and White Gate. Without them, we cannot have a strong, open, full, or clear heart. Love cannot be fully liberated or expressed until this important healing work is done. As Thornton Wilder wrote in *The Bridge of San Luis Rey,* "There is a land of the living and the land of the dead and the bridge is love, the only survivor, the only meaning."

the Gift
———

Dorothy Day was a lay activist who inspired many faith-based social and political change movements worldwide. She was famous for her wisdom, generosity, courage, and character. In her newspaper *The Catholic Worker,* she once expressed the essence of her life's work:

*The great need of the human heart is for love, and espe-
cially [for those] deprived of their own [people] to love.
Indeed, we know that the first commandment is to love,
and show our love . . . for our God by our love for our
fellows. And that is why a great emphasis must be placed
on . . . mercy.*

If we overcome fear and pride at the Black and White Gate, we receive plentiful wisdom gifts. Patience, tolerance, and compassion emerge, signaling that we have moved past fear and pride. Anger and arrogance diminish. Gratitude and forgiveness, the wisdom practices of the heart, release generosity of spirit and open the door for healing. The gifts of contrition, reparation, compassion, and mercy liberate the expressions of love and generosity that can begin to permeate and restore our relationships.

Reflections

Read and reflect daily on Jack Kornfield's "Prayer for Reconciliation." Notice at the end of each day if any changes have occurred, whether small or significant.

*May all mothers and sons be reconciled.
May all mothers and daughters be reconciled.
May all fathers and sons be reconciled.
May all fathers and daughters be reconciled.
May all sisters and brothers be reconciled.*

May all husbands and wives be reconciled.
May all partners and lovers be reconciled.
May all family members be reconciled.
May all employers and employees be reconciled.
May all community members be reconciled.
May all friends be reconciled.
May all women be reconciled.
May all men be reconciled.
May all men and women be reconciled.
May all religions be reconciled.
May all races be reconciled.
May all nations be reconciled.
May all peoples be reconciled.
May all creatures be reconciled.
May all beings of every form be reconciled.

Reflect on the following questions:

- What calls for forgiveness, reparation, and reconciliation in your life?
- With whom can you harness the power of genuine apology and let reconciliation work begin? What broken relationships need mending?
- What forgiveness do you need to extend to yourself?
- What harm have you done to others, and how can you rectify that harm?
- What forgiveness have others requested from you?

- Where do you struggle with fear and pride in your relationships, your work, your creativity?

Reflect daily on the relationships for which you are grateful. Extend an act of generosity or gratitude to a stranger, an acquaintance, or a loved one.

Practice

When we can hold opposing qualities within our nature in responsible and balanced ways, we develop personal character and increase our relationship skills. For example, if we can stay in a committed relationship without becoming excessively dependent, and remain free without being irresponsible or negligent, we stretch our capacity for developing character; we become more effective in all our relationships.

Our negative and positive shadows represent those aspects of ourselves that we dislike and often project onto others, and those desirable qualities we have not yet accepted or integrated. In order to do shadow work, we must first recognize that all the qualities we see in others are already present within ourselves. As we integrate all these qualities, they can come into the light. Once we acknowledge them, we can befriend them and discover new ways to be in relationship.

Integrating the shadows adds dimension to who we are. Use David Richo's table every day for twenty days, using one line as a practice for each day. See which of the opposites is the most difficult for you to hold. When does fear or pride obstruct your ability to hold both aspects simultaneously? Write down the insights that emerge.

Practice of Befriending the Shadow

Can I be		*While still remaining*
Committed in a relationship	1	Free
Angry at someone	2	Loving toward this person
Aware of my faults	3	High in self-esteem
Against an idea or plan	4	Respectful and cooperative
In agreement	5	Firm in my own conviction
Respectful and yielding	6	Firm in my own beliefs
A preserver of what is useful in a belief system	7	Free to disregard what no longer works for me
A parent or spouse	8	True to a career or hobby
Repelled by what someone does	9	Caring about the one who did it
Generous	10	Self-nurturing
Emotionally involved	11	Intellectually clear
Proud of someone	12	Aware of the person's shortcomings
Available for others	13	Able to preserve time for myself
Flexible	14	True to my standards
Able to see the worst possibilities	15	Hopeful
Able to take risks	16	Safety conscious
Responsibly in control of myself	17	Spontaneous
Limited in my commitment	18	Unconditionally loving
Afraid	19	Capable of acting
Honest in my persona	20	At work on my shadow

What stories and memories all feet hold
of life's mysterious journey.

Anonymous

the Rustic *gate*

Creativity, Service, and Generativity

Where the spirit

does not work with the hand,

there is no art.

Leonardo da Vinci

In beauty may I walk.

All day long may I walk.

Through the returning seasons may I walk.

On the trail marked with pollen may I walk.

With grasshoppers about my feet may I walk.

With dew about my feet may I walk.

With beauty may I walk.

With beauty before me, may I walk.

With beauty behind me, may I walk.

With beauty above me, may I walk.

With beauty below me, may I walk.

With beauty all around me, may I walk.

In old age wandering on a trail of beauty, lively, may I walk.

In old age wandering on a trail of beauty, living again, may I walk.

It is finished in beauty.

It is finished in beauty.

Navajo Blessing Way Prayer

Still bearing fruit in old age,

still remaining fresh and green.

Psalms 92:14

T he Rustic Gate is made of weathered wood and etched with distinctive designs that echo patterns found in nature. The gate opens to a vast green meadow flanked by high mountains. In the middle of the meadow, the creative fire burns—a fire that takes no wood. A gnome sits on a boulder near the fire. He wags his finger and says, "You'll never find your way out of here unless you tend to the creative fire, and leave behind work that is connected to your life dream."

At the Rustic Gate, we explore meaningful work, service, and creativity. Here we reexamine our connection to these, and reassess our life callings. The major questions for us to consider are: Are we doing work that serves others or generates a meaningful legacy? If not, why not? What do we want to contribute to this world? As we rediscover our interests and passions in work and service at this gate, we are guided, in the words of the Persian poet Rumi, to "let the beauty of what we love be what we do." Without this rediscovery, we will be prone to depression, stagnation, and despair.

the Task

The Rustic Gate is the gate of generativity. To generate is to initiate, to inspire, and to originate something that is meaningful, hopeful, and sustainable for ourselves and others. In generativity, we become mentors and stewards. We give back to our families and communities, sharing our wisdom, experience, and passion, and leaving a legacy. These are the tasks at this gate. In his book *The Creative Age,* Dr. Gene Cohen cites many exemplary individuals who, because they were driven by meaning rather than ambition, allowed their creativity and contributions to flourish well beyond the age of fifty. One such example was the Basque dramatist José Echegaray y Eizaguirre (1833–1916), who began his career teaching mathematics, but in later years found his true creative outlet in writing. He acquired literary fame through his many plays, and was genuinely surprised and delighted to receive the Nobel Prize for Literature at the age of seventy-one.

Maggie Kuhn, who founded the Gray Panthers in the 1970s, was outraged at the United States' mandatory retirement age of sixty-five. She was determined to end gerontophobia, the fear of old people and of growing old. She believed it was important to stay vital and creative at all ages. In an interview in *The Ageless Spirit,* she said, "Creativity and the joy of creativity are reinforced by new ideas. We must always be open to each new day, to the future, to new opportunities. They're there, but we have to be ready to see them."

Studies conclude that fostering our creativity in old age benefits us in the following ways:

- Creativity strengthens our morale later in life.
- It contributes to physical health as we age.
- It enriches relationships.
- It is our greatest legacy.

The Rustic Gate requires that we remain connected to our creative fire, the fire that will sustain our health and well-being. This fire has to be rooted in meaning and generativity, especially after age fifty, or it will not be sustainable. Marie Knowles of Portland, Maine, who is 104 years old, demonstrates a philosophy that resists anything fixed, obstructive, or unresolved. Her view of life is: "Pick out the fine things in life, and if you can't find them there, pick them out of your own head."

As we age, if we do not do meaningful work, any one of the following three obstacles identified by Dr. Cohen—fixed psychological patterns, fixed ideas, and unresolved family and social situations—will prevent our full creative expression and mire us in depression. The challenge at this gate is to consciously identify and overcome these obstacles. When we have done so successfully, repressed creative forces are liberated and can be used and expressed in our work, relationships, and service.

At the Rustic Gate we need to honestly review our work and service, and discover where our creative passion is released. Important questions surface at this gate to challenge us to reconsider how we spend our time and energy. What aspects of our lives are asking us to reconnect to the creative fire? How many projects have we completed in our lives? Which ones are unfinished? What have we contributed to our world, our community, and our family that makes a difference? What experience and wisdom will be irrevocably lost if we fail to transmit it? Where do we expend our energy in meaningful work? In what ways do we bring beauty into the world by what we create or generate?

Our work here is to connect with beauty, a major source of creativity and generativity. Beauty feeds the soul, and the soul feeds the creative fire. Medieval religious philosopher Thomas Aquinas suggested that three things are required to create beauty: *integritas* (wholeness), *consonantia* (harmony), and *claritas* (radiance). Japanese master artist Katsushika Hokusai (1760–1849) believed his art, creativity, and happiness improved with age because his love of the beauty and the majesty of Mount Fuji continued to inspire him. His most notable works, *Thirty-Six Views of Mount Fuji,* are the color prints he created between the ages of sixty-six and seventy-six. Hokusai's images of Mount Fuji achieved all three characteristics of sublime beauty: wholeness, harmony, and radiance. Like Hokusai, Paul Cézanne was inspired in his art by nature's beauty. Cézanne, one of the greatest post-Impressionist painters, was a champion of beauty, and believed that "art is a harmony parallel with nature."

In later life, our creativity, generative energy, and meaningful service compel us to make contributions that are sustainable, whole, harmonious, and deeply satisfying to the soul. Canadian painter Emily Carr said that the ultimate creative challenge of her life was to face old age and death, and to pass on what she loved about art. For her, it was important to be an example for younger artists, rather than a rival. She did not want to succumb to competition, comparison, and selfishness. Instead, she saw facing old age as the spiritual task of pacing, conserving her energy and strength as long as possible, and leaving a heritage of experience, skill, and wisdom to others. Carr wrote *Hundreds and Thousands: The Journals of an Artist* as her legacy, and was adamant that "old age without spirituality would be a ghastly trial." In her later years, she turned to nature as her spiritual solace. She loved sketching in the woods, and used her fiery generativity to mentor younger artists.

Mother Teresa is a superb example of someone who believed that life should be lived creatively and fully. Before she died at age eighty-seven, she had committed the last twenty years of her life exclusively to service — taking care of the sick, poor, and dying. Every day she was a model of her philosophy that true service comes from deep faith, silence, and love. Her life was her message. The ultimate task at the Rustic Gate is to create, generate, and serve meaningfully so that our lives can become our message.

the Challenge

In *The Wheel of Time,* Carlos Castaneda said, "To be young and vital is nothing. To be old and vital is sorcery." How do we vigilantly sustain and conserve our vitality as we grow older? The Rustic Gate challenges us to learn to access our natural generative energy. Stagnation, despair, boredom, loneliness, or indifference may signal that our generative energy is blocked. These experiences are referred to as acedia, from the Greek word *a-kedos,* "not caring" or sour. The Chinese written word for "boredom" consists of two characters, one for heart, and the other for killing. Boredom and apathy kill the human heart, and open the door to acedia. Thomas Aquinas defined acedia as the lack of energy to look at new things, and Hildegard von Bingen recognized the impact of acedia when she talked about the soul being weakened by coldness, indifference, and neglect. When asked about his approach to life in *Seasons of the Heart,* Vaclav Havel, former president of the Czech Republic, said, "I am not an optimist, because I am not sure that everything ends well. Nor am I a pessimist, because I am not sure everything ends badly. I just carry hope in my heart." Joy, hope, and possibility banish acedia and fuel generativity.

Matthew Fox made an important contribution to identifying the deadly sins of our time in his book *Sins of the Spirit, Blessings of the Flesh,* which reveals the major barriers to creativity. He says that many are extensions or aspects of acedia: lack of passion, dissipation of energy, misdirected love, and self-imposed isolation.

Erik Erikson, in his developmental model of human nature (summarized on the next few pages), notes that the later years require cultivation and expression of generativity and integrity, or the opposite states of stagnation and despair will manifest. Erickson examines these states from the perspectives of involvement, relationships, mental attitudes, physical image, and vocations.

Adulthood / Maturity Characteristics

Generativity / Integrity		*Stagnation / Despair*
Energy, motivation, mental growth, other absorbed, establishment of the next generation through altruistic and creative acts aligned with meaning and integrity	**Involvement**	Boredom, mental decline, self-absorbed, narcissistic self-indulgence
Growing, selfless, giving, involved in the life of the community	**Relationships**	Deteriorating, selfish, taking

Open, flexible, growing, creative	**Mind**	Closed, rigid, stuck
Realistic body image, balance	**Physical**	Unrealistic body image, imbalance
Sense of being needed, ongoing sense of exploration and discovery, daily contribution to life and others, generativity, character development	**Vocation**	Disillusionment, boredom, no sense of contribution to others, stagnation, loss of memory

The Four Rivers

Many traditional societies believe that the Four Rivers of Life—Inspiration, Challenge, Surprise, and Love—sustain and support us, and connect us to great gifts. They also believe that if we fail to stay connected to these rivers, we succumb to "walking the procession of the living dead" and begin to experience soul loss, depression, stagnation, or other manifestations of acedia.

The River of Inspiration reveals where we are in touch with our creative fire and our life dream. Any time that we experience expansion or hope, or feel uplifted, we are in the presence of creativity. As long as we can still be inspired, we know we are alive, refusing to join the procession of the living dead.

The River of Challenge calls us to stretch and grow beyond what is knowable or familiar. We notice who or what is asking us to leave our comfort zones and explore uncharted creative areas or interests. This river always asks us to move past any fixed notion of what we can do. If we are willing to be challenged, to become explorers again, acedia cannot come into our lives.

The River of Surprise keeps us fluid and flexible, and requires us to open to options and possibilities that we may not have considered. The Inuits have a saying about it: "There are two plans for every day, my plan and the Mystery's plan." This river reveals where we have become rigid or controlling rather than curious, flexible, and ready to trust what emerges for our consideration. The River of Surprise shows us where our attachments repress the natural flow of creativity and generativity.

The River of Love shows us where we are touched and moved by life's experience. If we are not, especially in our work, we know acedia is present and our heart has begun to close. Humor, joy, laughter, and love are considered medicines for the heart by some indigenous peoples. This river indicates that the work and service we love can make us happy. Kahlil Gibran reminds us of the value of service: "Work is love made visible."

How will we use our generative energies and stay connected to the Four Rivers of Life? This is the challenge of the Rustic Gate.

the Gift

The wisdom gift at this gate is generativity: the capacity to guide the next generation by engaging in meaningful altruistic acts carried out with integrity. Basque philosopher Miguel de Unamuno (1864–1936) describes the potent legacy that we leave in the hearts of those touched by our contribution long after we are gone: "Our greatest endeavor is to make ourselves irreplaceable . . . no one else can fill the gap that will be left when we die." This gift is a growing, selfless, creative involvement in community life and service. We harvest what we have sown, reflect upon our contribution, and consider what still yearns to be expressed within us.

Generativity gives us new meaning and purpose in the second half of life. We experience liberation from the three obstacles to our full creative expression — fixed psychological patterns, fixed ideas, and unresolved family and social situations — that are the doors to acedia. Instead we shift our commitment and allegiance to the Four Rivers of Life. As a result, our actions are brought into focus and our creative contributions can align with what is truly important.

Reflections

Before we create, there is always a period of reflection and incubation during which we let our creative ideas germinate and gestate until they can be brought fully into the world. It can be an internal process or take such external forms as writing, journaling, drawing, or creating a collage.

Spend fifteen minutes in silent meditation or take a walk while reflecting on one of the following questions. Notice what is revealed to you.

- What or who affirms your creative fire and generative spirit?
- With which of the Four Rivers of Life are you most comfortable or least comfortable: the River of Inspiration, the River of Challenge, the River of Surprise, or the River of Love?
- What contributions that you have made throughout your life have been meaningful and satisfying? What

are you consistently generating that comes from your passion? Recall Kahlil Gibran's words, "work is love made visible."

- What triggers the experience of acedia within you, or where do you currently find it present in your life?
- What provides you with hope? How do you foster and inspire hopefulness in others? Hope and imagining possibilities keep us from experiences of acedia. Often where there is hope, there is the presence of creativity and generativity.
- Who are the people who have most inspired you? How have they affirmed your creativity and encouraged you to exceed your perceived creative capacity? The word "inspire" comes from in-spirit; where are you "in spirit" with your creativity?

Practice

The practices of creativity are engaging and often take us to states of being in which we feel alive, full of joy, and inspired. When we fully engage our life force and take action, a generating quality occurs where one project or idea leads to others. We can become stuck when we fail to recognize that creativity is a process, and that the goal is only a part of the process. Ben Rail, who is ninety-two, is a remarkable example of someone who continues to overcome the obstacles to creativity. He does not believe in retirement; he retired three or four times and did not like it. He is a model of the spirit of generativity and continues to contribute to his community. Ben shared his love for creativity in *What's Worth Knowing* in this way:

> *I rode rodeo for five years, had my own welding business, even ran a doughnut shop until the war came and they started rationing oil and sugar. I've dabbled a little in just about everything. I'd always had a hankering to get my hands into some clay, but I didn't get a chance until now. I turned eighty-nine and opened up a ceramics studio. Lots of people come to my shop, work on their projects, and have a good time. Meanwhile, I'm making a few dollars, and my supplies are all paid for. You can't beat that. I just don't believe in retirement.*

Remember Ben Rail's words as you consider the following:

- Where have you "retired" prematurely or settled for less in your life? What interests have you put aside, saying, "When I have time or enough money, I may do this . . ." Write them down and review your list. Are there any whose time has come?
- Each week, do something that is fun and brings the spirit of laughter and play into your life. Joy fuels creativity and nourishes the soul.
- Practice bringing curiosity and openness to the unexpected and unfamiliar. Let yourself approach a

new experience as an adventure, and learn everything you can about it.

• Extend generosity of spirit in each possible moment at home, at work, in the community, and in relationships. Look for ways you can be helpful or alleviate stress or suffering for another through compassionate service.

Redeem me and be gracious to me.

My foot stands in a straight place.

Psalms 26:11–12

the Bone *gate*

Authenticity, Character,
and Wisdom

*With the bones of my fingers,
I touched a fragile beauty that reflected
the soul's winged nature.*

Anonymous

From the cowardice that shrinks from new truth,

From the laziness that is content with half-truths,

From the arrogance that thinks it knows all truth,

O God of Truth, deliver us.

An ancient scholar

It is not by muscle, speed, or physical dexterity that
great things are achieved, but by reflection, force of character,
and judgment; in these qualities old age is usually
not only not poorer, but it is even richer.

Cicero

The Bone Gate brings us to the "bones of who we are"—a metaphor for our authentic self. This gate strips away and shreds what is disingenuous in our nature, and any false remnants are burned to ashes. It requires congruence among all aspects of our true self, and we undergo a test to see if we have integrated the faces that we uncovered at the White Picket Gate: child, youth, adult, elder, and essence. The Bone Gate urges us to develop character, integrity, and wisdom. Here we find ourselves strongly attracted to those who embody these traits. We are reminded of Gertrude Stein's words, "No one real is boring."

At the Bone Gate, we must release denial and indulgence, competition and comparison, and seduction and strategizing for personal gain, all of which are barriers to authenticity. In addition, we must free ourselves from anything that contributes to cynicism. It is a major obstruction to the development of character.

the Task

The primary task at this gate is to embody the authentic self and the wisdom found in our character, to be, as Gandhi said, "valiant in spirit." To do this, we assess our character honestly, and face both the positive and negative consequences of our choices, actions, and behaviors. Here, we finally summon the courage to risk telling the truth about who we are and are not. The primary questions at this gate are: How and why do we avoid being who we truly are? What gets in the way of trusting ourselves completely? Under what circumstances do we deceive ourselves?

When we are phony, pretentious, or cynical in order to achieve interpersonal or material gain, we diminish ourselves and disrespect others. The extent to which we have positive regard and respect for ourselves and others determines how successfully we achieve congruity among all aspects of our character. At the Bone Gate, we develop the self-regard to be true to who we are, unwilling to compromise our integrity in order to satisfy the expectations of others or win their approval. We know our behavior is authentic when we can consistently *say what we mean, do what we say, and say what's so when it's so.* We can check ourselves by asking whether our motivation, speech, appearance, and actions match our true character in all the varied aspects of our lives — relationships, work, and community. When our words and actions are in harmony, wisdom and authenticity emerge.

Authenticity is the expression of what is genuine and natural. It commands great respect because, unfortunately, it is so rare. The desire to be accepted, or to engage in competition and comparison, drives us to limit our behavior to what falls within narrowly prescribed, predictable norms. The Bone Gate breaks down all such affectations and pretenses.

In our later years, wisdom can only be expressed in tandem with authenticity and character. Minnie Nighthawk, who at age eighty-seven is described as looking both young and old, spoke about making a habit of honesty in *What's Worth Knowing:*

> *When I was a girl, my father taught me how to hunt,*
> *saying a woman should know how to take care of herself.*
> *My dear mother taught me two lessons—to eat breakfast*
> *in the morning, and to make honesty a way of life. Both*
> *should happen every day, she said, not become things you*
> *choose now and then. Dishonest situations give you lots*
> *of stress in life. Think about how hard it is to remember*
> *when and where you lied about something, and what ex-*
> *actly you said. It gives you a headache. I've had very little*
> *stress because I learned so early to tell the truth. I haven't*
> *had to worry about keeping things straight. That is why*
> *I have so few wrinkles.*

The Guarani Indians of South America believe that those who lie and squander their words betray the soul. In the Guarani language, *NÈ ê* means both "word" and "soul." When we lie, we shake trust, generate stress, lose self-esteem, and corrupt our character. Dishonesty and deception may provide a short-term solution, but in the long term, they contribute to soul loss and taint our integrity.

Ridding ourselves of old patterns and accessing the authentic self are entryways to freedom and the domain of wisdom. In fact, as we discover how to befriend these processes, aging and renewing our character can be what Carl Jung called a "winter grace." Jung believed that if we do not develop inner strength as we age, we will become defensive, dogmatic, depressed, resentful, and cynical.

At the Bone Gate, we realize that our homeland of authenticity is within, and there we are sovereign. Until we rediscover this ancient truth in a way that is unique for each of us, we are condemned to wander, seeking solace in the outer world where it cannot be found.

In *At Seventy,* writer May Sarton recounted how, during a poetry reading at a Connecticut college, she mentioned, "This is the best time of my life — I love being old." Someone challenged her and asked loudly, "Why is it good to be old?" Sarton answered, "Because I am more myself than I have ever been. There is less conflict. I am happier, more balanced . . . and more powerful . . ."

the Challenge

The Bone Gate calls for us to face and break through two illusions that keep narcissistic self-importance and self-deception in place: that other people are responsible for our happiness, and that we can change them. These illusions profoundly impact the dynamics of our relationships with others. When we expect others to make us happy or we are invested in changing them, we enter relationships for selfish, arrogant, and immature reasons. In both instances, other individuals are seldom seen or appreciated for who they are. Instead, they are rendered as objects whose purpose is to serve our narcissistic needs. When we release these two illusions, our relationship dynamics change, and we become more self-sufficient, collaborative, and interdependent. We also find that other temptations and illusions are tested and begin to unravel.

According to Billy Mills and Nicholas Sparks's book *Wokini*, the Native American Lakota tradition teaches that during initiatory processes, Iktumi, the trickster or liar figure, tempts us with eight lies that keep us from accessing our true nature and attaining what is meaningful and spiritually satisfying:

> *If only I were rich, then I would be happy.*
> *If only I were famous, then I would be happy.*
> *If only I could find the right person to marry, then I*
> *would be happy.*
> *If only I had more friends, then I would be happy.*
> *If only I were more attractive, then I would be happy.*
> *If only I weren't physically handicapped in any way,*
> *then I would be happy.*
> *If only someone close to me hadn't died, then I would*
> *be happy.*
> *If only the world were a better place, then I would*
> *be happy.*

In truth, none of these self-deceptions has any relationship to happiness, and in fact they present overwhelming barriers to authenticity. Ever the trickster, Iktumi tells us that if we obsessively strive for as many of the eight illusions as we can in every aspect of our lives, we will become happy and successful. But in fact, once we attain these goals, we are bewildered to find ourselves still without satisfaction, meaning, or happiness. Only when we cease to chase after these illusions will we become liberated from our own fears, frantic strivings, false beliefs, and attachments.

Whether we are prepared for it or not, the Bone Gate will show us the self-deception of Iktumi's illusions. The issue at this gate is to realize that we can accomplish nothing meaningful during the second half of life unless we reject the eight lies and reconnect our search for happiness with values that support our character and moral fiber. Only then can we assume the wisdom mantle of the elder and become a resource of compassion, insight, and clarity.

The Four Essential Bones

Indigenous peoples say that in order to return to our true nature, we must befriend four essential symbolic bones in our body: the *backbone,* a metaphor for courage; the *wishbone,* which represents our lives' wishes, hopes, and dreams; the *funny bone,* a symbol of our sense of humor, which keeps us resilient and flexible; and finally the *hollow little bone,* which allows the Mystery to work us rather than us trying to work the Mystery. A traditional greeting among Appalachian Mountain people reveals the meaning of the hollow bone. They ask, "What's learnin' ya? What's workin' ya?" The hollow little bone reminds us that the Mystery is learning us and working us rather than the other way around.

At the Bone Gate we ask ourselves: Which of these four bones, with its essential character and qualities, needs strengthening or realigning?

- Backbone — the quality of courage, to stand by one's heart or core

- Wishbone — the quality of hope, to stay open to dreams, blessings, and possibilities
- Funny bone — the quality of humor, to foster joy and maintain flexibility
- Hollow bone — the quality of trust, to maintain openness, curiosity, and faith

As we age, we need all four bones to fully develop our character, dispel cynicism, and cultivate wisdom. How do we cultivate wisdom? Where do we find wisdom expressed in the world? Spiritual traditions teach that it can be found in silence, nature, solitude, the wisdom of elders, ourselves, and reflection on the nature of life and death. Will we choose instead to forfeit wisdom for Iktumi's eight lies? Will we refuse the invitation to come home to our true nature? In our later years, the price of self-deception, self-sabotage, and resisting character development is too high. Our authentic selves beckon, and we strive to earn the great compliment that Emerson extended to a colleague: "Who you are . . . thunders so loud that I cannot hear your words."

the Gift

As we honestly confront our deceptions of self and others, the wisdom gifts that emerge at this gate are authenticity, honesty, and integrity — all essential qualities of character development. At the Bone Gate, consistency among intention, word, and action shows that personal authenticity is aligned with the four bones. As we use our discernment, and our wisdom increases, we become responsible for fully engaging in life rather than merely rehearsing it. In William Maxwell's book, *The Letters of Sylvia Townsend Warner,* he quotes Sylvia Townsend Warner's experience of when she felt connected to life in an authentic and wise way and when she did not:

> *I think as one grows older one is appallingly exposed to wearing life instead of living it. Habit, physical deterioration and a slower digestion of our experiences, all tend to make one look on one's dear life as a garment, a dressing gown, a raincoat, a uniform, buttoned on with recurrent daily [tasks]. . . . [F]or myself I found one remedy, and that is to undertake something difficult, something new, to re-root myself in my own true faculties. . . . For in such moments, life is not just a thing one wears, it is a thing one does and is.*

She reminds us that wisdom grows out of a life rich in experience, meaning, and challenges. We accumulate wisdom with age as long as we are deeply engaged, and continue to learn about ourselves, others, and the world around us. T. S. Eliot expresses this in his poem "East Coker": "Old men ought to be explorers." Through our explorations later in life, we can come to know what is important in our character. At the Bone Gate we experience what James Hillman wrote in his book *The Force of Character*: "Character begins to govern life's decisions evermore pertinently, and permanently. Values come under more scrutiny, and qualities such as decency and gratitude become more precious than accuracy and efficiency."

Reflections

In order to develop character, we need sincere honest reflection upon what is not working in our lives. This is the process of uncompromising self-assessment and self-confrontation: the willingness to face what is superfluous or fabricated within our nature.

Reflect upon the eight lies of Iktumi:

> *If only I were rich, then I would be happy.*
> *If only I were famous, then I would be happy.*
> *If only I could find the right person to marry, then I would be happy.*
> *If only I had more friends, then I would be happy.*
> *If only I were more attractive, then I would be happy.*
> *If only I weren't physically handicapped in any way, then I would be happy.*
> *If only someone close to me hadn't died, then I would be happy.*
> *If only the world were a better place, then I would be happy.*

- Which of these eight lies have you been telling yourself, and for how long? What impact have they had on you, your work, and your loved ones?
- What lies have you initiated or colluded in for the sake of being included or being seen as special?
- Where is cynicism present in your life?

- What actions can you take to break through the two primary illusions of life: that someone is responsible for your happiness, and that you have the ability to change others?
- What triggers your need to diminish or inflate your self-worth?
- What do you trust unshakably in yourself? This is the foundation where character, wisdom, and authenticity reside.
- When and with whom are you completely yourself, without fabrication or pretense?
- What are the benefits of coming fully into your authentic self and bringing your gifts into the world?

Practice

Reclaiming the authentic self and developing character are essential tasks in the second half of life. Congruence within our nature fosters authenticity. Acting with integrity is the practice that brings us into alignment and congruence.

People who have character and are honest say what they mean, do what they say, and say what's so when it's so. For three weeks, practice saying only what you mean, doing everything you say you'll do, and saying what's so as soon as you know it to be so. Write down what you discover about the integrity of your words, actions, and timing, and in which of these you find yourself consistently challenged or falling short. This daily practice will strengthen courage and truth-telling, and will reduce misunderstanding and conflict in your life.

The practice of being authentic requires us to release outdated or unnecessary patterns and beliefs. It takes daily discipline to stay connected to the four bones. Which of your four bones, each with its essential character qualities, needs strengthening or realigning? Take an action every day for six months to develop the four qualities equally.

- Back bone: the quality of courage. Speak a truth that is difficult for you to say.
- Wish bone: the quality of hope. Take a step toward realizing a dream.
- Funny bone: the quality of humor. Identify a way in which you take yourself too seriously. See if you can instead approach it lightheartedly.
- Hollow bone: the quality of trust. Identify something you take on faith. See if you can extend that feeling of openness to another area of your life.

People in some traditional societies believe that when they keep shameful secrets or deceive themselves and others, they cut their power in half. Many of them speak their deceptions and shameful secrets aloud to a tree or large boulder, or they mark a leaf or twig representing a secret and bury or burn it, vowing not to deceive anyone or keep shameful secrets from that day forward. The Lakota Sioux use their traditional sweat lodge ceremony for purification and say the following prayer to restore their character and integrity: "Endurance, cleanliness, strength, purity, will keep our lives straight, our actions only for a good purpose. Our words will be truth. Only honesty shall come from our interaction with all things." Develop your own ritual to reinforce your courage and honesty and to help you release patterns of deception.

Anointed feet, blessed feet—
purified and restored in their integrity.

Anonymous

the Natural *gate*

The Presence of Grace:
Happiness, Satisfaction, and Peace

*A bit of fragrance
always clings to the hand
that gives you roses.*

Chinese proverb

I wish you health.

I wish you wealth

That passes not with time.

I wish you long years.

May your heart be as patient as the earth

Your love as warm as the harvest gold.

May your days be full, as the city is full

Your nights as joyful as dancers.

May your arms be as welcoming as home.

May your faith be as enduring as God's love

Your spirit as valiant as your heritage.

May your hand be as sure as a friend

Your dreams as hopeful as a child.

May your soul be as brave as your people

And may you be blessed.

Wigilia Blessing

There is something healing
in the repeated refrains of nature—
the assurance that dawn comes after night,
and spring after the winter.

Rachel Carson
The Sense of Wonder

The Natural Gate is found in deep dark woods surrounded by a beautiful desert. In the heart of the woods, an elm tree and an ash tree form an arch. It is said that all the women of the world come from the elm and all the men come from the ash. Here is where we find deep contentment and satisfaction. All the happy moments of our lives are found at this gate, which is illuminated by natural light.

At the Natural Gate, we are encouraged to come home to our natural rhythm and our internal sanctuary. Here, we contemplate the ways we experience deep peace, balance, and equanimity in our lives. Wherever we reside naturally and with ease, happiness and peace flourish in our being. We cross the threshold of the Natural Gate when we stop expecting the external world to meet our needs and instead get in touch with our internal natural resources. Through silence, contemplation, and reflection, we befriend and embrace solitude. We create a sanctuary where fountains of contentment and satisfaction overflow, and we experience spiritual solace. A sense of peace unrelated to action is found at this gate, and we harvest deep meaning from our experiences.

the Task

At the Natural Gate, our work is to come home to ourselves and discover where we are truly content, happy, and satisfied. These states show us where deep self-acceptance resides and where we trust our natural being and our inner wilderness. The most splendid external expression of that wilderness is nature itself. Nature, in its majestic beauty, can put our soul at ease, relax us, and deliver us to a timeless mystery that opens the doors to contemplation, reflection, integration, and transformation. When we experience inner quiet and peacefulness, we can savor the wisdom and spirituality found in nature, in silence, and in precious moments we experience at the center of our being.

the Power *of* Nature

Many indigenous cultures and spiritual traditions recognize four natural sanctuaries where we can remember and come home to who we are: the desert, the mountains, the waters, and the woods. Nature comes from the Latin *natus,* "to be born." Native peoples look to these places for remembrance, soul retrieval work, and to be reborn or renewed. Because we are made from the natural elements — fire (our energy), air (our breath), water (our blood), and earth (our bones) — we are always drawn to come into harmony with the beauty of nature around us. It nourishes the soul and opens us to be born into the mysterious presence and promptings of our own vast inner world.

Because we have originated from nature, if we wander away for too long, its rhythm and beauty always call us to return to it. Vietnamese spiritual teacher Thich Nhat Hanh tells us what happens when we do not stay connected to the land. "Nature is our mother. If we live cut off from her, we get sick." In our later years, there is a deep desire to simplify our lives and to return to the enjoyment of our childhood explorations of the natural world. We recognize that it feeds our souls.

Throughout history, in all cultures and on all continents, artists, poets, musicians, and writers, striving to lead us to the transcendent, have attempted to capture the beauty of nature, and to put into images, words, or songs that which is inexpressible. Yet many ordinary individuals who live close to the earth and nature's seasons, such as farmers, weavers, or fishermen, witness daily the integration of the ordinary and transcendent in their own lives and communities. Novelist D. H. Lawrence's sanctuary for self-exploration and connection to nature was the forest and deep woods. In his *Studies in Classic American Literature,* he honored what he consistently found there:

> *This is what I believe.*
> *That I am I.*
> *That my soul is a dark forest.*
> *That my known self will never be more than a little*
> *   clearing in the forest.*
> *That gods, strange gods come forth into the clearing of*
> *   my known self, and then go back.*

That I must have the courage to let them come and go.
That I will never let mankind put anything over me, but
that I will try always to recognize and submit to the
gods in me and the gods in other men and women.

Lawrence recognized the importance of "strange gods" coming forth to reshape and renew us and help us attain growth and liberation. The desire to replenish, rebalance, and come into inner harmony and natural rhythm is a universal longing that spans time and traditions. We can nourish it in nature.

Just as Lawrence loved the woods, Pearl Buck felt that rivers, springs, and brooks offered the only peace and contentment that could sustain her in her later years. Jacques Cousteau, the French oceanographer, felt that the sea was a spiritual sanctuary and warned about *ivresse des grandes profondeurs*—the intoxication of the great depths. Those who have felt the presence of the sacred in the desert include artist Georgia O'Keeffe and writer Barry Lopez. Both of them have loved its vast spaciousness and found humility and spiritual strength there. Jesus, Buddha, and Mohammed all spent extended time in the desert.

Mountains and wilderness called to photographer Ansel Adams. Noted poet Robinson Jeffers wrote of the spiritual integrity of the mountains. Leonardo da Vinci believed that those not connected to nature lived an empty life. He wrote, "Those who took as guide anything other than nature herself, the teacher of teachers, labored in vain." Among others who were taught by nature were Emerson, Thoreau, Mary Oliver, and Annie Dillard; all were fortified by nature's ability to bring grandeur, solace, comfort, dramatic beauty, and spiritual meaning into their lives.

In traditional societies of North America, individuals who are in transition go on vision quests, spending time alone in nature without diversions. This allows them to go within, listen deeply for guidance, and reflect upon what is true and right for their spiritual development and life purpose. Narritjin Maynuru Yirrkala, an Australian Aborigine, said, "We long to see the ground. It is our power. And we must stay close to it or maybe we will get lost."

the Solace *of* Silence

The Natural Gate requires us to touch our spiritual life so that we may flourish in the gardens of silence, solitude, stillness, and simplicity. It reminds us that through these practices, we can replenish ourselves and open to grace. No time spent in wordless solitude is ever wasted. Meister Eckhart was convinced that "the most powerful prayer . . . and the worthiest work of all is the outcome of the quiet mind. . . . To the quiet mind all things are possible." Most spiritual practices involve what Browning called "opening out a way whence the imprisoned splendor may dart forth."

What practices help us find comfort and solace? What is our relationship to silence? How can we make time for contemplation and reflection?

Francis of Assisi reminds us of the essential task at this gate:

> *What is it that stands higher than words? Action.*
> *What is it that stands higher then action? Silence.*

the Challenge

The Natural Gate challenges us to slow down. When we are overly busy and live at an unnaturally fast pace, this gate escapes our attention and we are unable to pass through it. Those who are most active often have the greatest need for time alone. Winston Churchill, a man who was as active as any in the twentieth century, knew how important quiet and solitude were for nourishing himself. Even in the midst of running a nation during a terrible world war, he never missed his time alone each day so that internally he would be rested and renewed.

Another challenge at the Natural Gate is learning the difference between being alone and loneliness. Being alone without the comforts offered by silence and nature can generate isolation, depression, or loneliness. Thomas Merton reminds us that "to live a spiritual life we must find the courage to enter the desert of our loneliness and to change it by gentle and persistent efforts into a garden of solitude." A colleague whose wife had died told me, "When loneliness haunts me, maybe I can look at it as a threshold instead of a dead end, or a meeting place instead of a gray, bottomless pit — then maybe I won't live in a frenzy of activity all the time." Two weeks later he signed up for a meditation retreat to begin learning how to transform loneliness into solace.

The last challenge at this gate is to regain our sense of humor in order to cultivate the experience of joy and happiness through laughter, playfulness, and the capacity to celebrate. Our inability to open to humor shows us where we have lost perspective, where we are attached to certain outcomes, and where we are disconnected from the spirit of joy. "Joy is the fruit of the spirit," says the New Testament, and it is one of the fruits to reclaim in our later years at this gate. The Koran speaks to us of the power of laughter: "He who makes his companions laugh, deserves paradise." Native Americans believe that laughter is a medicine for the heart and cultivates joy. We need to consider who and what make us happy, and who and what make us laugh. They are healing agents in our lives.

Theodor Seuss Geisel began writing his Dr. Seuss stories at fifty-three, and at seventy wrote *You're Only Old Once.* He believed that laughter and creating amusing characters and situations were the best ways to stay happy and flexible in his later years. He was awarded a Pulitzer Prize at age eighty for his wit and wisdom. The comedian Victor Borge said that laughter was the shortest distance between two people. Laughter lightens our burdens, releases our attachments, and restores balance. It provides a shared experience of joyous connection between people and dispels isolation. Whenever we experience happiness and peace, we are at the gate where the medicines of laughter, joy, and fun can flourish.

the Gift

At the Natural Gate, we begin to experience the wisdom gifts of peace, balance, and equanimity. From the beauty of the time that we spend in nature and the mystery that we find in the sweet territory of silence, we draw a primal comfort, solace, and grace that deepen our connection to our inherent spirituality. *Ridhwan* is an Arabic word for reaching a sense of deep peace and balance in life; it means satisfying, satisfied, fulfilling, fulfilled, and making content or contented.

It conveys both a state of being and an action: being that acts, acts by its very being. It is the perfect term to describe the fruits found at the Natural Gate.

In many spiritual traditions, this experience of fulfillment or contentment is synonymous with the experience of grace, which is another wisdom gift gleaned at the Natural Gate. Grace fosters peace and faith, and restores balance. It opens the door to equanimity, and dispels loneliness and isolation. Grace returns us to joy, the fruit of our spirit.

Thomas Merton wrote, "May we all grow in grace and peace, and not neglect the silence that is printed in the center of our being. It will not fail us." Nor will the beauty and majesty of nature.

Reflections

The rhythms and cycles of nature are intertwined with our rhythms and cycles. As children, we may have spent a great deal of time outdoors in the elements, playing on the earth or in the water and fully breathing the air around us. As adults we spend more time indoors and less in nature. In our later years, we need to balance the time we spend indoors and outdoors to come fully into our own rhythm.

Nature's rhythm is medium to slow. Few creatures move rapidly in nature unless they are in danger. Many of us live in the fast lane, out of nature's rhythm. There are two things we can never do in the fast lane: we can neither deepen our experience nor integrate it, both essential tasks in the second half of life. Silence and nature foster an environment in which we can do this work and nurture our spirit.

Reflect on the following questions:

- What is your current relationship to nature? What aspects of nature do you love the most — the mountains, deserts, waters, or woods?
- At this time in your life, what is your relationship to silence, solitude, stillness, and simplicity? Where do you find solace and comfort?
- Who are the healing agents in your life? Where do you find joy — "the fruit of the spirit" — in your life?
- What takes you away from living a more balanced and fulfilling life?
- Who or what are your current sources of happiness, satisfaction, contentment, and peace?

Write in your journal about times or situations during which you have experienced grace, peace, and faith.

Practice

When we lose touch with the rhythms of nature, we become unbalanced. To be fully present within our nature, we must be in balance with the land around us. We benefit by taking time from our daily routines of work, relationships, and other commitments to return to nature. It provides a way to renew ourselves.

- Spend an hour outdoors every day.

- Spend at least a half hour every day in silence, to deeply listen to the center of your being. As Merton said, it will not fail you. If you are willing to enjoy the sweet territory of silence, you will experience solace and peace found nowhere else, and freedom from anxiety.

- Notice and give gratitude for all that makes you happy and brings joy into your life and for the grace and peace in your life and within your own nature.

- Set aside one full day each month to spend in silence or nature. Notice your experience and the changes you undergo, internally and externally.

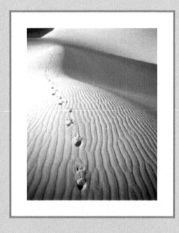

The first dream of God is the wilderness

which he spreads at our feet.

C. A. Meier
A Testament to the Wilderness

the Gold *gate*

Nonattachment, Surrender,
and Letting Go

Then I must know that still I am in the hands
of the unknown God,
he is breaking me down to his new oblivion
to send me forth on a new morning, a new man.

D. H. Lawrence
Shadows

When the signs of age begin to mark my body

(and still more when they touch my mind);

when the ill that is to diminish me or carry me

off strikes from without

or is born within me;

when the painful moment comes in which I

suddenly waken

to the fact that I am ill or growing old;

and above all at the last moment when I feel I am losing hold of myself

and am absolutely passive within the hands

of the great unknown forces that have formed me;

in all those dark moments, O God,

grant that I may understand that it is you

(provided only my faith is strong enough)

who are painfully parting the fibers of my being

in order to penetrate to the very marrow of my

substance

and bear me away within yourself.

Pierre Teilhard de Chardin

From the unreal lead me to the real.

From darkness lead me to light

From death lead me to immortality.

The Upanishads

A t last we arrive at the Gold Gate, which is glowing and bathed in a numinous light. This is where we awaken to the deepest core of who we are, and are asked to let go and trust our own spirituality. It is the gate of surrender, faith, and acceptance, where we learn to release and detach before beginning something new or progressing forward. It is the final gate in the initiatory process of the second half of life. It requires us to befriend the death of our physical form.

the Task

At the Gold Gate, we learn about nonattachment, the capacity to care deeply while remaining objective. We learn how to let go, and move into a deep acceptance of all that we have experienced. In our later years, we can no longer live with resignation — the ways that we have withdrawn, abandoned hope, and lost trust and the resolve to face important issues. Nor can we hold onto old disappointments and regrets. We let them go so we can befriend the culmination of our life. The Gold Gate provides us with the opportunity to develop a sense of mortality that is both realistic and positive. This can only happen through our "harvest," the fulfillment that comes from knowing that our lives have meaning and significance.

At this gate, we will not be released until we have achieved closure for anything unfinished in our lives, and have satisfied our inner longings and deep callings. We begin to look at our lives objectively, free of paraphernalia, props, or ego. We reflect and ask ourselves the deepest questions: Have we loved well? Has our life been meaningful? Or, as Jim Harrison asked in his book *Off to the Side*:

> *What are the peculiar landscapes of mind that fueled the decisions behind how I lived my life, and what were the largely unconscious impulses? When you map your life in retrospect is there a bit of a blind cartographer at work? Simply enough, what did I do with my time?*

Honorable Closure

The practice of honorable closure brings us to the completion and release of our relationships, our health, our creative works, our desires, our disappointments, and our lifelong dreams. It allows us to befriend our mortality, the ultimate task at this gate.

Many traditional societies believe that if you end your work and relationships well, new and greater blessings and opportunities will arise. When there is honorable closure, there are no regrets. In cultures around the world, honorable closure is achieved by expressing gratitude for the people and situations that have helped us or challenged us to grow, and by identifying any remaining regrets.

The Gold Gate shows us where we have unfinished personal or interpersonal business; it also requires us to deepen our detachment, acceptance, and surrender in order to meet our true nature, which rises from the hidden depths of our being. At this gate, we discover that our invisible spiritual nature is a real presence. This is where we learn and live the difference between *knowing about* the Mystery and *knowing from direct experience of* the Mystery, as we approach our passage, stewarded by death, into the great unknown.

the Challenge

As we look back on our lives, we realize that the harvest of youth is achievement, the harvest of middle age is perspective, and the harvest of old age is wisdom. The Gold Gate reminds us that wisdom is a process, not an outcome. It is within most of our grasps because it depends more on learning from our daily life experiences than on native ability or attaining a certain age. Wisdom grows with trust, clarity, and curiosity, and dwindles with control or attachments. At the Gold Gate, we are finally called upon to release any clever coping strategies or impulses to control that remain, and stop the limiting patterns and behaviors that have kept our attachments in place. Nonattachment, befriending our mortality, calling upon our ancestors, and attending to our spirituality indicate ways we are cultivating wisdom.

The Work of Nonattachment

The benefits of nonattachment are many. It opens the door to unconditional love. It implies deep faith and trust in life that allow relationships and events to unfold without interference or control. It is not to be confused with indifference or lack of caring, nor is it a deficiency of commitment. Instead, it is the practice of compassionate acceptance, even in the face of strong desire or strong aversion. Through nonattachment we feel honored, respected, and free to be ourselves.

Nonattachment to outcome is central to real satisfaction and acceptance. Nothing suffocates the life force more thoroughly than trying to control what is happening. Rather than trying to assert control over relationships, health, work, or any other aspect of life where we do not trust, we need to know that in the situations that are important to us, we have planned and prepared well. Then we can be open to possibilities and outcomes that we may not have considered.

As we release critical judgments, we can honestly accept our circumstances rather than merely resign ourselves to them. This surrender into our own lives allows us to release our beliefs about what we think our lives should be.

Spiritual teacher Ram Dass discovered an unshakable clarity, realignment, and radical shift to nonattachment after his stroke. In his book *Still Here,* he described the stroke as

> . . . a samurai sword, cutting apart the two halves of my life. It was a demarcation between two stages. In a way, it's been like having two incarnations in one: this is me, that was "him.". . . Seeing it that way saves me from the suffering of making comparisons, of thinking about the things I used to do but can't do anymore because of the paralysis in my hand.

Like Ram Dass, we learn in our later years that it is not the event but how we respond to the event that is important.

Pain, Suffering, and Loss

Dr. Albert Schweitzer, who worked for decades in Africa with the sick and dying, said that dying itself was not feared as much as pain or suffering: "Pain is a more terrible lord of mankind than even death itself, and awakens us to a courage and faith unrealized before." In the second half of life at the Gold Gate, if we have not done so already, we begin to learn from both our suffering and from one of life's most challenging teachers: pain.

Here we rediscover our lifelong relationship to emotional, physical, mental, and spiritual pain as we grieve for and cope with the loss of our capacity to work, the loss of loved ones, and the decline of our own health. We also lose the most painful illusion of all, that this physical life will go on forever. When pain appears, it generally takes over to the extent that we may completely lose ourselves in it and forget all else. The fear that arises around pain and loss is often worse than the pain itself. Pain is one of the most challenging issues at the Gold Gate because it signals the poignant and fleeting nature of our life.

However, if we can befriend pain, it can be our greatest ally. It can teach us patience, compassion, strength in vulnerability, and the ability to live fully and wholeheartedly within our limitations. It can even teach us to let go of the fear of pain itself. Eventually we can become detached from pain, being with it but not encumbered by it, and able to be much more of who we are. Pain teaches us that to continue living is always a choice, moment to moment, and the value we get from life is always connected to the value we give to ourselves and others. Pain leads us to the source of our courage, the center of our faith, and trust in the people who share this journey with us.

Staying United with Our Ancestors

The Gold Gate gives us the opportunity to connect to our ancestors. Some native traditions see ancestor spirits (family members or loved ones) as important teachers of nonattachment because they have faced the process of letting go and have experienced the ultimate unknown, the mystery of death. During our later years, memories and dreams of our deceased family members and loved ones become more vivid and frequent. Often, they occur as a way to prepare and comfort us by letting us know that others have gone before us and are still remembered long after they have physically departed. Basque philosopher Miguel de Unamuno describes the importance of deeply rooted ancestral connections and the help they provide: "All my ancestors live undiminished in me and will continue to live, united with me, in my descendants."

Befriending Death

At the Gold Gate, late in life we learn to befriend death and prepare for its arrival. We acknowledge that we have been born, lived, learned, and loved. We accept our losses, the roads unexplored, the people we miss, and the dreams unfulfilled; we begin to make peace with all that is in and around us. We reject nothing and cling to nothing. We simply observe the ebb and flow of our life.

We practice the art of dying while we live, experiencing endings when we say good-bye to people who will be separated from us for a time, or when we complete something that has significance. Every night we practice letting go when we release ourselves to sleep and the mysterious place of dreams, trusting that we will return. In these small daily actions, we prepare for what is required at our death. In her book *Companion Through the Darkness*, Stephanie Erickson says,

> *It seems that we are humbled before the great events of life. Events over which we have no power, no influence. Events that do not play fair. To be humbled like this is not meant to be punishment, but rather Death grooming us to awaken.*

Spiritual Awakening and Care

The end of life is a deep inner quest that moves in cycles of high and low. Understanding this adds resiliency to our way of approaching the gifts and challenges that the second half of life presents. The major challenge at the Gold Gate is to recognize spiritual issues as they emerge in preparation for our final passage.

Zen Hospice of San Francisco has pioneered an end of life program sponsored by the Metta Institute to help people experience death as a spiritual process of emergence. This work reminds us of our inherent spirituality and its many forms. Spirituality, which gives meaning to life, is often expressed in religious terms but can also be found in nature, silence, work, art, music, family, and friendship. It can bring wholeness to the emotional, physical, and intellectual dimensions of life. The spirit is the essence of the person, what makes us unique. As we deal with illness and dying, we often cope with questions about meaning and purpose: Why did this happen to me? Why now? As we struggle through these questions, dying can be a time of great potential for renewal and an opportunity to find meaning in life. But facing these questions may also result in spiritual distress, which surfaces as doubt, uncertainty, anxiety, and sadness. Whatever supports our sense of faith helps us make the transition from such despair to peaceful acceptance.

The essence of our spiritual history emerges at the Gold Gate in the beliefs, fears, dreams, and struggles that surface uniquely to each of us during the process of dying. We live in a society that keeps death at arm's length and fosters two of the greatest fears associated with death: isolation and not being treated normally. It is important to honor the dying person's preference, whether it is for connection or solitude, rather than imposing or assuming that we know what that person wants. Our greatest challenge at the Gold Gate is to have the courage to face whatever suffering, sadness, or pain may come during this ultimate spiritual process called dying. Here we awaken to a courage and faith unrealized before.

the Gift

The Gold Gate offers the wisdom gifts of freedom and liberation. Nonattachment, surrender, and acceptance foster our deliverance, while courage and faith strengthen our capacity to face our own suffering, pain, or sadness as we prepare to enter the gateless gate. Theologian

Mary Reuter says that we can experience fearlessness through three layers of detachment: detachment from material gain, detachment from self-importance, and detachment from the urge to control or dominate others. To hold onto nothing is the root of happiness and peace. If we allow ourselves to rest here, we find that it is a tender, open-ended place. This is where the path of fearlessness leads, and where we rest in expanded, unlimited peace.

Reflections

Nonattachment, surrender, and letting go of the future are necessary if you are to reflect on your entire life and all that you have been and done, and enter the final threshold of your life. You make the conscious choice of living not in the past or future, but in each present moment. This takes great courage and the ability to make peace with your life: to live without hope or fear, to let go without regret, to know that you have lived fully.

- Reflect on your life and notice the areas where you are attached or have unfinished business. Consider this: If you knew when your life would end, what would you do to live out your final days in a full and complete way? As you cannot know the moment your life will end, why not live each moment as though it were the most precious one left to you?
- How do you honor your ancestors? What do you know about them? What qualities in your ancestors would you like to emulate?

- What was your first experience of death? Who died? What impact did this event have upon you? How has your relationship to death changed since then?
- Identify what you are grateful for in your life journey; what have you learned from this journey and what have been the many blessings and opportunities offered to you along the way?
- Review where you have been positively affected and changed for the better by your life journey.
- Where were you challenged, tested, and stretched beyond your perceived capacities?
- What do you need to mend in your life or where do you need to do rectification or reparation work? What final forgiveness work is needed for you to feel complete? What do you need to say or do to feel complete?

Practice

Many cultures have practices associated with surrender at the end of life. Death is seen not as finality, but as the greatest transformation since birth. It is also a cause to celebrate those who have lived well, had an effect on their families and communities, and left a legacy for future generations.

Consider the uniqueness and impermanence of human life that carries the certainty of death for us all. What legacy will you leave for future generations? How will you be remembered? How do you want to be remembered? Write a draft of your desired obituary. Prepare your own memorial. As you do these practices, what is revealed to you about what is meaningful for you in your life and how you want to be remembered?

Use your own death as a teacher, a companion who is always with you, who reminds you to live your life fully every day, for it may be your last. This in itself is a rigorous practice; although you *know* you are going to die at some unknown hour or day, you do not *believe* it. Remember the last words of Robert Louis Stevenson: "If this is death, it is easier than life."

What attachments do you find in your personal life? Professional life? Spiritual life? Consider Mary Reuter's three layers of release from attachment: from material gain, from self-importance, and from the urge to control or dominate others. Which of these will you practice releasing this year?

Create a Book of Revelations; include your favorite memories, turning points, epiphanies, peak experiences, synchronicities, prayers, spiritual practices, significant moments, and important dreams.

Give me, good Lord

Glorious God, give me grace to amend my life, and to have an eye to my end without begrudging death, which to those who die in you, good Lord, is the gate of a wealthy life.

And give me, good Lord, a humble, lowly, quiet, peaceable, patient, charitable, kind, tender and pitiful mind, in all my works and all my words and all my thoughts, to have a taste of your holy, blessed Spirit.

Give me, good Lord, a full faith, a firm hope, and a fervent charity, a love of you incomparably above the love of myself.

Give me, good Lord, a longing to be with you, not to avoid the calamities of this world, nor so much to attain the joys of heaven, as simply for love of you.

And give me, good Lord, your love and favour, which my love of you, however great it might be, could not deserve were it not for your great goodness.

These things, good Lord, that I pray for,
give me your grace to labour for.

Sir Thomas More, 1478–1535

The feet of him that bring good tidings,

that announce peace . . .

that announce salvation.

Isaiah 52:7

After
the
Eight Gates

We all come in through the
Silver Gate and we all go out
through the Gold Gate.
There are many gates in between . . .

After going through the eight gates of initiation in the second half of life, we can no longer deny that our relationship to time, people, places, work, spirituality, and our own lives changes significantly. A precious immediacy surfaces as we finally realize that our remaining time is limited. We find ourselves compelled to use it well and wisely. We begin actively to align our priorities and responsibilities to serve what has heart and meaning for us. We are drawn to revisit old memories, people, and places that we left long ago, coming back full circle to experiences we must integrate rather than avoid.

The eight gates emphasize the poignancy of time and the need to integrate all aspects of our lives' experience. As we passed through each gate, we were presented with its specific tasks, challenges, gifts, reflections, and practices. These provided a necessary structure to help us identify and reassess what and whom we cherish, what is truly important to us, and what we deeply value. They also revealed what we choose to mend, redo, or correct in our lives, and what longings we have yet to satisfy.

Which gates, in particular, evoked unexpected feelings, dreams, memories, longings, and callings for you? Which gates were the most inspirational, challenging, or surprising? It may already be evident to you which gates you want to revisit for additional inspiration or deepening work. Or you may want to work with each gate again, by yourself or with friends and family, as an eight-month practice.

Regardless of how you choose to further engage this initiatory process, what changes or actions are you going to undertake as a result of what surfaced for you as you experienced each gate? How will you live a meaningful life with the time you have remaining? What contributions are still important for you to make?

What is the most important thing to remember as we move towards the end of our journey? Ralph Waldo Emerson said it best: "To leave the world a bit better, whether by healthy child, a garden patch, or redeemed social condition; to know even one life has breathed easier because you live — that is to have succeeded."

My hope for us is that our journey through the mysteries of the second half of life will provide a meaningful retrospective and compelling incentive to embrace elderhood with dignity, grace, wisdom, and unlimited generativity. May we all remember that to leave the world a better place for future generations is to have lived a meaningful life, and to have succeeded.

May your journey be
blessed and protected always.

Photo Acknowledgments *and* Permissions

Photo Acknowledgments

Author photo by Marianne Gontarz York. Photos of hands on pages xvi, xvii, 21, 27, 43, 57, 71, 89, 105, 121 and 135, and on the book cover are reprinted with the permission of the photographer, Penny Bauer. This series is from a project called "A Circle of Gifts: The Wisdom of Older Women," copyrighted by Penny Kaela Bauer, The Gifts Project, PO Box 1485, Langley, WA 98260, 360-221-8512, www.thegiftsproject.com.

The author and publisher gratefully acknowledge the permission to use quotations or passages as indicated below. In every case regarding permission, diligent efforts were made to obtain permission to reprint selections from previously published works. In a few instances, permission was not received in time for formal acknowledgment. Any omission will be corrected in future printings upon notification. All published citations are documented and formally cited and listed in the bibliography.

Pre-Introduction

Anne Sullivan Macy, "Hands." Source: Houston, Jean, *Public Like a Frog: Entering the Lives of Three Great Americans.* Wheaton, IL: Quest Books, 1993, p. 199. Reprinted by permission of Jean Houston.

Sir Laurens van der Post. Source: Lemle, Mickey, *Hasten Slowly: The Journey of Sir Laurens van der Post* (VHS). New York: Lemle Pictures, Inc., 1996.

Threshold Work at the Eight Gates

Shinsho. Source: Stryk, Lucien, and Takashi Ikemoto, trans., *Zen Poems of China and Japan: The Crane's Bill.* New York: Grove Press, 1973, p. 7. Reprinted by permission of Grove Press.

Basarab Nicolescu. Source: *Parabola: Myth, Tradition, and the Search for Meaning. Miracles,* vol. 22:4 (Winter 1997), p. 65.

Henry Wadsworth Longfellow. Source: Mabey, Juliet, *God's Big Book of Virtues.* Boston: Oneworld, 1998, p. 100.

Mircea Eliade. Source: *Parabola: Myth, Tradition, and the Search for Meaning. Threshold,* vol. 25:1 (Spring 2000), p. 70.

Pierre Teilhard de Chardin, *The Divine Milieu.* New York: Harper & Row, 1960, p. 80.

Rumi. Source: Moody, Harry R., and David Carroll, *The Five Stages of the Soul: Charting the Spiritual Passages That Shape Our Lives*. New York: Anchor Books, 1997, p. 41.

Carl Jung. Source: Wilhelm, Richard, trans., *The Secret of the Golden Flower: A Chinese Book of Life*. Orlando, FL: Harcourt, Brace & Co., 1962, p. viii.

Basho. Source: McGinn, Florence, *Blood Trail*. www.insynthesis.com/reviews, Feb. 7, 2004.

The Eight Gates of Initiation in the Second Half of Life

Eva Pierrakos, *The Pathwork of Self-Transformation*. New York: Bantam, 1990, p. xvi. Reprinted by permission of Bantam Books.

The Silver Gate

Ellen Bass, "To Praise," in *Cries of the Spirit: A Celebration of Women's Spirituality*, ed. Marilyn Sewell. Boston: Beacon Press, 1991, p. 207.

Yom Kippur prayer. Source: Roberts, Elizabeth, and Elias Amidon, eds., *Life Prayers From Around the World*. San Francisco: HarperSanFrancisco, 1996, p. 33.

Martin Buber. Source: Cousineau, Phil, *Once and Future Myths: The Power of Ancient Stories in Modern Times*. Berkeley, CA: Conari Press, 2001, p. 157.

John O'Donohue, "Fluent," *Conamara Blues*. New York: HarperCollins, 2001, p. 23. Reprinted by permission of HarperCollins Publishers Inc.

Leo Tolstoy, *A Confession*. Source: Moody, Harry R., and David Carroll, *The Five Stages of the Soul: Charting the Spiritual Passages That Shape Our Lives*. New York: Anchor Books, 1997, pp. 88–92.

William Butler Yeats. Source: Hirsch, Edward, *The Demon and the Angel: Searching for the Source of Artistic Inspiration*. New York: Harcourt, 2002, p. 71.

Clarissa Pinkola Estés, *Women Who Run With the Wolves*. New York: Ballantine Books, 1992, p. 400.

Federico Garcia Lorca. Source: Hirsh, Edward, *The Demon and the Angel: Searching for the Source of Artistic Inspiration*. New York: Harcourt, 2002, p. 71.

Martha McCallum. Source: Lustbader, Wendy, *What's Worth Knowing*. New York: J.P. Tarcher/Putnam, 2001, p. 76.

Moody, Harry R., and David Carroll, *The Five Stages of the Soul: Charting the Spiritual Passages That Shape Our Lives.* New York: Anchor Books, 1997, p. 8.

The White Picket Gate

Rainer Maria Rilke. Source: Barrow, Anita, and Joanna Macy, eds., *Rilke's Book of Hours.* New York: Riverhead Books, 1996, p. 122. © 1996 by Anita Barrows and Joanna Macy. Used by permission of Riverhead Books, an imprint of Penguin Group (USA) Inc.

Plotinus, *The Enneads,* ed. Stephen MacKenna. London: Faber & Faber, 1956. Source: www.ccat.sas.upenn.edu/jod/texts/plotinus, Aug. 26, 2004.

Nicolas of Cusa. Source: *Parabola: Myth, Tradition, and the Search for Meaning. Fear,* vol. 23:3 (Fall 1998), pp. 30–31.

Thomas Browne. Source: John Cook, ed. *The Book of Positive Quotations.* Minneapolis: Fairview Press, 1997, p. 183.

George Ivanovitch Gurdjieff. Source: Ouspensky, P. D., *In Search of the Miraculous.* New York: Harcourt Brace Jovanovich, 1949, p. 240.

Carl Jung. Source: Richo, David, *Shadow Dance: Liberating the Power and Creativity of Your Dark Side.* Boston: Shambhala Publications, 1999, p. 1.

David Richo, *Shadow Dance: Liberating the Power and Creativity of Your Dark Side.* Boston: Shambhala Publications, 1999, p. 108.

Sue Monk Kidd, *When the Heart Waits.* Reprint, San Francisco: HarperSanFrancisco, 1992, p. 8.

Hui-Neng. Source: www.wikipedialorg/wiki/Koan, Aug. 4, 2004. Quote is a fragment of case #23 of the *Wu-Men Kuan.*

The Clay Gate

Taisen Deshimaru. Source: www.QuoteWorld.org, Aug. 2003.

Kuan Tao-sheng. Source: Karasu, T. Byram, *The Art of Serenity.* New York: Simon & Schuster, 2003, ch. 1. Reprinted by permission of Simon & Schuster.

Care Story. Source: Leonard, Linda Schierse, *The Call to Create: Celebrating Acts of Imagination.* New York: Harmony Books, 2000, p. 79.

Walt Whitman, *Leaves of Grass.* Boston: Modern Library, 1921, p. 194.

Eduardo Galeano, *Walking Words.* New York: W.W. Norton & Co., 1993, p. 151.

Margaret Fowler. Source: *Seasons of the Heart: Men and Women Talk About Love, Sex and Romance After 60.* Novato, CA: New World Library, 2000, p. 36.

Myrlie Evers-Williams, *Watch Me Fly.* Boston: Little, Brown & Co., 1999. Source: www.angelesarrien.com, Feb. 2003.

Robin Morgan, "The Network of the Imaginary Mother," in *Cries of the Spirit: A Celebration of Women's Spirituality,* ed. Marilyn Sewell. Boston: Beacon Press, 1991, p. 213.

The Black and White Gate

Edwin Markham, "Outwitted," in *The Book of Love: A Treasury Inspired by the Greatest of Virtues,* ed. Andrew M. Greeley and Mary G. Durkin. New York: A Forge Book, published by Tom Doherty Associates, 2002, p. 24.

The Siddur of Shir Chadash. Source: Roberts, Elizabeth, and Elias Amidon, eds., *Life Prayers From Around the World.* San Francisco: HarperSanFrancisco, 1996, p. 261.

M. C. Richards, *Centering: In Pottery, Poetry, and Person.* Middletown, CT: Wesleyan University Press, 1964, p. 54.

The Dalai Lama. Source: www.dailycelebrations.com. Search Dalai Lama, July 2004.

Carl Jung. Source: Schechter, Howard, *Jupiter's Rings: Balance From the Inside Out.* Ashland, OR: White Cloud Press, 2002, p. 82.

Marge Piercy, "To Have Without Holding," *The Moon Is Always Female.* New York: Alfred A. Knopf, a division of Random House, 1980, p. 40.

Roger Walsh, *Essential Spirituality: The Seven Central Practices to Awaken Heart and Mind.* New York: John Wiley & Sons, Inc., 1999, p. 81.

Rumi. Source: modern translation of Kabir Helminski, *The Rumi Collection. From Mathnawi* V, 588–590. Boston: Shambhala, 2000, p. 162.

Zalman Schachter-Shalomi and Ronald S. Miller, *From Age-ing to Sage-ing: Profound New Vision of Growing Older.* New York: Warner Books, 1995, p. 99. © 1995 by Zalman Schachter-Shalomi and Ronald S. Miller. Reprinted by permission of Warner Books.

Thorton Wilder, *The Bridge of San Luis Rey.* Cutchogue, NY: Buccaneer Books, 1991, p. 196.

Dorothy Day. Source: Rifkin, Ira, ed., *Spiritual Innovators: Seventy-Five Extraordinary People Who Changed the World in the Past Century.* Woodstock, VT: Skylight Paths Publishing, 2002, p. 174.

Jack Kornfield, "Prayer for Reconciliation," *The Art of Forgiveness, Lovingkindness, and Peace.* New York: Bantam Books, 2002, p. 63. © 2002 by Jack Kornfield. Used by permission of Bantam Books, a division of Random House.

Practice and chart of befriending the shadow. Source: Richo, David, *Shadow Dance: Liberating the Power and Creativity of Your Dark Side.* Boston: Shambhala Publications, 1999, pp. 248–249.

The Rustic Gate

Leonardo da Vinci. Source: Boldt, Laurence, *Tao of Abundance.* New York: Penguin, 1999, p. 257.

Navajo Blessing Way Prayer. Source: www.unityofflagstaff.org/prayers/Navajo, Oct. 10, 2004.

Rumi. Source: Barks, Coleman, trans., *The Essential Rumi.* Edison, NJ: Castle Books, 1997, p. 36.

Gene Cohen, *The Creative Age: Awakening Human Potential in the Second Half of Life.* New York: Avon Books, 2000, pp. 110, 165.

Maggie Kuhn. Source: Berman, Phillip L., and Connie Goldman, eds., *The Ageless Spirit.* New York: Ballantine Books, 1992, p. 130.

Marie Knowles. Source: Perls, Thomas T., and Margery H. Silver, with John F. Lauerman. *Living to 100: Lessons in Living to Your Maximum Potential at Any Age.* New York: Basic Books, 1999, p. 87.

Thomas Aquinas. Source: www.Sr.McBride, Aug. 4, 2004. © Sr. Thomas Mary McBride, O.P. 2002, version July 27, 2002. *Summa Theologiae,* 1a, 39, 8.

Paul Cézanne. Source: www.nitaleland.com/quotations/naturequotes.htm, Jan. 2004.

Emily Carr. Source: Leonard, Linda Schierse, *The Call to Create: Celebrating Acts of Imagination.* New York: Harmony Books, 2000, pp. 238–239.

Carlos Castaneda, *The Wheel of Time: The Shamans of Mexico, Their Thoughts About Life, Death, and the Universe.* New York: Washington Square Press, 2001.

Thomas Aquinas on acedia and Hildegard von Bingen on acedia. Source: Fox, Matthew, *Sins of the Spirit, Blessings of the Flesh: Lesson for Transforming Evil in Soul and Society.* New York: Harmony Books, 1999, pp. 167–168.

Vaclav Havel. Source: Gross, Zenith Henkin, *Seasons of the Heart: Men and Women Talk About Love, Sex, and Romance After 60.* Novato, CA: New World Library, 2000, p. 243.

Matthew Fox, *Sins of the Spirit, Blessings of the Flesh: Lesson for Transforming Evil in Soul and Society.* New York: Harmony Books, 1999, p. 77.

Erik Erikson. Source: Fowler, James W., *Stages of Faith: The Psychology of Human Development and the Quest for Meaning.* San Francisco: HarperSanFrancisco, 1995, pp. 42–51.

Inuit saying. Source: Oral tradition from author's collection of research.

Kahlil Gibran. Source: www.columbia.edu/~gm84/gibran7.html, Jan. 2004.

Miguel de Unamuno. Source: Hillman, James, *The Force of Character and the Lasting Life.* New York: Ballantine, 1999, p. 200.

Ben Rail. Source: Lustbader, Wendy, *What's Worth Knowing.* New York: Jeremy P. Tarcher/Putnam, 2001, pp. 60–61.

The Bone Gate

Ancient scholar quote. Source: Ryan, M. J., ed., *A Grateful Heart.* Berkeley, CA: Conari Press,1994, p. 206.

Cicero. Source: Cohen, Gene, *The Creative Age: Awakening Human Potential in the Second Half of Life.* New York: Avon Books, 2000, p. 21.

Gertrude Stein. Source: From the author's collection.

Minnie Nighthawk. Source: Lustbader, Wendy, *What's Worth Knowing.* New York: Jeremy P. Tarcher/Putnam, 2001, pp. 178–179.

Carl Jung. Source: Pipher, Mary, *Another Country: Navigating the Emotional Terrain of Our Elders.* New York: Riverhead Books, 1999, p. 188.

May Sarton. Source: Gross, Zenith Henkin, *Seasons of the Heart: Men and Women Talk About Love, Sex, and Romance After 60.* Novato, CA: New World Library, 2000, pp. 213–214.

Billy Mills and Nicholas Sparks, *Wokini: A Lakota Journey to Happinesss and Self-Understanding.* New York: Orion Books, 1990, p. 36.

Sylvia Townsend Warner. Source: Maxwell, William, *The Letters of Sylvia Townsend Warner.* New York: Norton & Co., 1982, pp. 267–268.

T. S. Eliot, "East Coker," *Four Quartets,* www.tristan.icom43.net/quartets/coker. html, July 2004.

James Hillman, *The Force of Character and the Lasting Life.* New York: Ballantine, 1999, p. 55.

The Natural Gate

Chinese proverb. Source: Greenberg, Joseph, ed., *Universals of Language.* Boston: MIT Press, 1966, pp. 163–164.

Wigilia Blessing. Source: Radlowski, Roger Jan, and John J. Kirvan, *The Spirit of Poland.* Minneapolis: Winston Press, 1980, p. 6.

Rachel Carson, *The Sense of Wonder.* New York: HarperCollins, 1965, p. 38.

Thich Nhat Hanh. Source: Zubko, Andy, *Treasury of Spiritual Wisdom: A Collection of 10,000 Inspirational Quotations.* San Diego, CA: Blue Dove Press, 1998, p. 330.

D. H. Lawrence. Source: Schechter, Howard. *Jupiter's Rings: Balance From the Inside Out.* Ashland, OR: White Cloud Press, 2002, pp. 97–98.

Pearl Buck. Source: Zubko, Andy, *Treasury of Spiritual Wisdom: A Collection of 10,000 Inspirational Quotations.* San Diego, CA: Blue Dove Press, 1998, p. 438.

Jacques Cousteau. Source: Ferrucci, Piero, *Inevitable Grace: Breakthroughs in the Lives of Great Men and Women: Guides to Your Self-Realization.* Los Angeles: Jeremy P. Tarcher, 1990, p. 276.

Georgia O'Keeffe, and Barry Lopez. Source: Ferrucci, Piero, *Inevitable Grace: Breakthroughs in the Lives of Great Men and Women: Guides to Your Self-Realization.* Los Angeles: Jeremy P. Tarcher, 1990, p. 44.

Robinson Jeffers, *The Selected Poetry of Robinson Jeffers,* ed. Tim Hunt. Stanford, CA: Stanford University Press, 2001, p. 502.

Leonardo da Vinci. Source: Ferrucci, Piero, *Inevitable Grace: Breakthroughs in the Lives of Great Men and Women: Guides to Your Self-Realization.* Los Angeles: Jeremy P. Tarcher, 1990, p. 37.

Narritjin Maynuru Yirrkala. Source: Elkins, David N., *Beyond Religion: A Personal Program for Building a Spiritual Life Outside the Walls of Traditional Religion.* Wheaton, IL: Quest Books, 1998, p. 210.

Meister Eckhart. Source: O'Neal, David, ed., *Meister Eckhart, From Whom God Hid Nothing.* Boston and London: Shambhala Publications, 1996, p. 15.

Robert Browning, "Paracelsus." Source: Miller, Betty, *Robert Browning, A Portrait.* New York: Scribner, 1953, p. 273.

St. Francis of Assisi. Source: Zubko, Andy, *Treasury of Spiritual Wisdom: A Collection of 10,000 Inspirational Quotations.* San Diego, CA: Blue Dove Press, 1998, p. 428.

Thomas Merton. Source: Nouwen, J. M. Henri, *Reaching Out: The Three Movements of the Spiritual Life.* New York: Image Books, Doubleday, 1986, p. 34.

Thomas Merton. Source: Ryan, M. J., ed., *A Grateful Heart.* Berkeley, CA: Conari Press, 1994, p. 52.

C. A. Meier, *A Testament to the Wilderness: Ten Essays on an Address.* Santa Monica, CA: The Lapis Press, 1985, p. 139.

The Gold Gate

D. H. Lawrence. Source: Luke, Helen M., *Old Age: Journey Into Simplicity.* New York: Parabola Books, 1987, p. 101.

Pierre Teilhard de Chardin. Source: Oman, Maggie, ed., *Prayers for Healing: 365 Blessings, Poems, and Meditations from Around the World.* Berkeley, CA: Conari Press, 1997, pp. 239–240.

Upanishads, trans. Juan Mascero (Classic Series), New York: Viking Penguin, 1965, p. 165.

Jim Harrison, *Off to the Side, A Memoir.* New York: Atlantic Monthly Press, 2002, p. 100.

Nonattachment definition. Source: Schechter, Howard, *Jupiter's Rings: Balance From the Inside Out.* Ashland, OR: White Cloud Press, 2002, p. 161.

Ram Dass, *Still Here: Embracing Aging, Changing, and Dying,* ed. Mark Matousek and Marlene Roeder. New York: Riverhead Books, 2000, p. 185.

Albert Schweitzer. Source: From the author's collection.

Miguel de Unamuno. Source: Arrien, Angeles, *The Four-Fold Way: Walking the Paths of the Warrior, Teacher, Healer, and Visionary.* San Francisco: HarperSanFrancisco, 1993, p. 114.

Stephanie Erickson, *Companion Through the Darkness: Inner Dialogues on Grief.* New York: Harper Perennial, 1993, p. 69.

Metta Institute End of Life Program, Sausalito, CA, 415-888-2113, www. mettainstitute.org., Oct. 20, 2004; Zen Hospice Brochure, 2004.

Mary Reuter. Source: Kurtz, Ernest, and Katherine Ketcham, *The Spirituality of Imperfection: Storytelling and the Search for Meaning.* New York: Bantam, 1992, pp. 172–173.

Thomas More. Source: Morgan, Richard Lyon, *Fire in the Soul: A Prayer Book for the Later Years.* Nashville, TN: Upper Room Books, 2001, pp. 120–121.

After the Eight Gates

Ralph Waldo Emerson. Source: Kushner, Harold, *Living a Life That Matters.* New York: Random House, 2002, p. 157.

Bibliography

Almaas, A. H. *Diamond Heart, Book 1.* Berkeley, CA: Diamond Books, 1987.

Arrien, Angeles. *The Four-Fold Way: Walking the Paths of the Warrior, Teacher, Healer, and Visionary.* San Francisco: HarperSanFrancisco, 1993.

_____. *The Nine Muses: A Mythological Path to Creativity.* New York: Jeremy P. Tarcher/Putnam, 2000.

Aquinas, Thomas. *Basic Writings of St. Thomas Aquinas,* 2 vol. set. Indianapolis: Hackett Publishing, 1997.

Barks, Coleman. *Open Secret.* Putney, VT: Threshold Books, 1984.

_____. *Unseen Rain.* Putney, VT: Threshold Books, 1986.

_____, trans. *The Essential Rumi.* Edison, NJ: Castle Books, 1997.

Barrow, Anita, and Joanna Macy, eds. *Rilke's Book of Hours.* New York: Riverhead Books, 1996.

Berman, Phillip L., and Connie Goldman, eds. *The Ageless Spirit.* New York: Ballantine Books, 1992.

Boldt, Laurence. *Tao of Abundance.* New York: Penguin, 1999.

Boorstein, Sylvia. *Pay Attention, for Goodness' Sake: Practicing the Perfections of the Heart — The Buddhist Path of Kindness.* New York: Ballantine Books, 2002.

Brandt, Karen Nilsson, and Sharon Nederman. *Living Treasures: Celebration of the Human Spirit.* Santa Fe, NM: Western Edge Press, 1997.

Brewi, Janice, and Anne Brennan. *Mid-Life Spirituality and Jungian Archetypes.* York Beach, ME: Nicolas-Hays, 1988, 1999.

Bronfman, Edgar M. *The Third Act: Reinventing Yourself After Retirement.* New York: Putnam, 2002.

Campbell, Joseph. *The Hero With a Thousand Faces.* Princeton, NJ: Princeton University Press, 1973.

Carotenuto, Aldo. *Eros and Pathos: Shades of Love and Suffering,* trans. Charles Nopar. Toronto: Inner City Books, 1989.

Carpenter, Candice. *Chapters: Create a Life of Exhilaration and Accomplishment in the Face of Change.* New York: McGraw-Hill, 2002.

Carr, Emily. *Hundreds and Thousands: The Journals of an Artist.* Toronto: Stoddard Publisher, 1986.

Carson, Rachel. *The Sense of Wonder.* New York: HarperCollins, 1965.

Carter, Jimmy. *The Virtues of Aging.* New York: Ballantine, 1998.

Casarjian, Robin. *Forgiveness: A Bold Choice for a Peaceful Heart.* New York: Bantam Books, 1992.

Casey, Karen. *Keepers of the Wisdom: Reflections From Lives Well Lived.* Center City, MN: Hazelden, 1996.

Castaneda, Carlos. *A Separate Reality.* New York: Simon & Schuster, 1991.

——————. *The Wheel of Time: The Shamans of Mexico, Their Thoughts About Life, Death, and the Universe.* New York: Washington Square Press, 2001.

Chesterton, G. K. *Saint Francis of Assisi.* New York: Image Books, 1987.

Chinen, Allan B. *In the Ever After: Fairy Tales and the Second Half of Life.* Wilmette, IL: Chiron Publications, 1999.

Chödrön, Pema. *Comfortable With Uncertainty: 108 Teachings.* Boston: Shambhala, 2002.

Chödrön, Thubten. *Working With Anger.* Ithaca, NY: Snow Lion Publications, 2001.

Churchill, Winston. *Never Give In: The Best of Winston Churchill's Speeches.* New York: Hyperion Press, 2003.

Clift, Jean Dalby. *Core Images of the Self: A Symbolic Approach to Healing and Wholeness.* New York: Crossroad, 1992.

Cohen, Gene D. *The Creative Age: Awakening Human Potential in the Second Half of Life.* New York: Avon Books, 2000.

Collopy, Michael. *Architects of Peace: Visions of Hope in Words and Images.* Novato, CA: New World Library, 2000.

Cook, John, ed. *The Book of Positive Quotations.* Minneapolis: Fairview Press, 1997.

Cousineau, Phil. *Once and Future Myths: The Power of Ancient Stories in Modern Times.* Berkeley, CA: Conari Press, 2001.

Cousteau, Jacques Yves. *Jacques Cousteau: The Ocean World*. New York: Abrams, 1985.

Dalai Lama. *Ethics for the New Millennium*. New York: Riverhead Books, 1999.

Dass, Ram. *Still Here: Embracing Aging, Changing, and Dying*, eds. Mark Matousek and Marlene Roeder. New York: Riverhead Books, 2000.

de Unamuno, Miguel. *Tragic Sense of Life*. New York: Dover, 1954.

Dobisz, Jane. *The Wisdom of Solitude: A Zen Retreat in the Woods*. San Francisco: HarperSanFrancisco, 2004.

Dychtwald, Ken. *Healthy Aging*. Gaithersburg, MO: Aspen Publishers, 1999.

Dyer, Wayne W. *Wisdom of the Ages: A Modern Master Brings Eternal Truths Into Everyday Life*. New York: HarperCollins, 1998.

Eisler, Riane. *The Power of Partnership: Seven Relationships That Will Change Your Life*. Novato, CA: New World Library, 2002.

Eliade, Mircea. *The Sacred and the Profane*. New York: Harcourt Books, 1968.

Eliot, T. S. *Complete Poems and Plays*. New York: Harcourt, Brace, and World, 1962.

Elkins, David. *Beyond Religion: A Personal Program for Building a Spiritual Life Outside the Walls of Traditional Religion*. Wheaton, IL: Quest Books, 1998.

Ellmann, Richard. *Yeats: The Man and the Masks*. New York: W. W. Norton, 2000.

Erickson, Stephanie. *Companion Through the Darkness: Inner Dialogues on Grief*. New York: Harper Perennial, 1993.

Estés, Clarissa Pinkola. *Women Who Run With the Wolves*. New York: Ballantine, 1992.

Evers-Williams, Myrlie. *Watch Me Fly*. Boston: Little, Brown & Co., 1999.

Feldman, Reynold. *Wisdom: Daily Reflections for a New Era*. Winona, MN: Saint Mary's Press, Christian Brothers Publications, 2000.

Ferrucci, Piero. *Inevitable Grace: Breakthroughs in the Lives of Great Men and Women: Guides to Your Self-Realization*. Los Angeles: Jeremy P. Tarcher, 1990.

Fischer, Kathleen. *Winter Grace: Spirituality and Aging*. Nashville, TN: Upper Room Books, 1998.

Fowler, James W. *Stages of Faith: The Psychology of Human Development and the Quest for Meaning*. San Francisco: HarperSanFrancisco, 1995.

Fowler, Margaret. *Seasons of the Heart: Men and Women Talk About Love, Sex and Romance After 60.* Novato, CA: New World Library, 2000.

Fox, Matthew. *Sins of the Spirit, Blessings of the Flesh: Lesson for Transforming Evil in Soul and Society.* New York: Harmony Books, 1999.

Frantz, Dean L. *The Inner Journey: Lectures and Essays on Jungian Psychology.* Toronto: Inner City Books, 2000.

Galeano, Eduardo. *Walking Words,* trans. Mark Fried. New York: Norton, 1993.

Germer, Fawn. *Hard Won Wisdom: More Than 50 Extraordinary Women Mentor You to Find Self-Awareness, Perspective, and Balance.* New York: Berkley, 2001.

Gibran, Kahlil. *The Prophet.* New York: Random House, 1976.

Gignoux, Jane Hughes. *Some Folk Say: Stories of Life, Death, and Beyond.* New York: FoulkeTale Publishing, 1998.

Gimbutas, Marija. *The Goddess and Gods of Old Europe.* Berkeley: University of California Press, 1987.

Goldberg, Philip. *Roadsigns: Navigating Your Path to Spiritual Happiness.* Emmaus, PA: Rodale, 2003.

Gould, Roger. *Transformation: Growth and Change in Adult Life.* New York: Simon & Schuster, 1981.

Greenberg, Joseph, ed. *Universals of Language.* Boston: MIT Press, 1966.

Greeley, Andrew M., and Mary G. Durkin, eds. *The Book of Love: A Treasury Inspired by the Greatest of Virtues.* New York: A Forge Book published by Tom Doherty Associates, 2002.

Grof, Stan, and Christina Grof. *The Stormy Search for the Self: A Guide to Personal Growth Through Transformational Crisis.* Los Angeles: Jeremy P. Tarcher, 1992.

Groopman, Jerome. *The Anatomy of Hope: How People Prevail in the Face of Illness.* New York: Random House, 2003.

Gross, Zenith Henkin. *Seasons of the Heart: Men and Women Talk About Love, Sex, and Romance After 60.* Novato, CA: New World Library, 2000.

Harner, Michael. *The Way of the Shaman.* New York: HarperCollins, 1990.

Harris, Theodore F. *Pearl S. Buck: A Biography. Vol. 2. Her Philosophy as Expressed in Her Letters.* New York: John Day Co., 1969–1970. (out of print)

Harrison, Jim. *Off to the Side, A Memoir.* New York: Atlantic Monthly Press, 2002.

Hedva, Beth. *Betrayal, Trust, and Forgiveness: A Guide to Emotional Healing and Self-Renewal* (rev. ed.). Berkeley, CA: Celestial Arts, 1992, 2001.

Heilbrun, Carolyn G. *The Last Gift of Time: Life Beyond Sixty.* New York: Ballantine, 1997.

Helminski, Kabir. *The Rumi Collection.* Boston: Shambhala, 2000.

Hillman, James. *The Force of Character and the Lasting Life.* New York: Ballantine, 1999.

Hirsch, Edward. *The Demon and the Angel: Searching for the Source of Artistic Inspiration.* New York: Harcourt, 2002.

Hokusai, Katsushika. *Thirty-Six Views of Mount Fuji.* Japan: Weatherhill, 1993.

Housden, Roger. *Chasing Rumi: A Fable About Finding the Heart's True Desire.* San Francisco: HarperSanFrancisco, 2002.

Houston, Jean. *Public Like a Frog: Entering the Lives of Three Great Americans.* Wheaton, IL: Quest Books, 1993.

———————. *The Search for the Beloved.* Los Angeles: Jeremy P. Tarcher, 1997.

Izzo, John. *Second Innocence: Rediscovering Joy and Wonder.* San Francisco: Berrett-Koehler, 2004.

Jaffe, Lawrence W. *Celebrating Soul: Preparing for the New Religion.* Toronto: Inner City Books, 1999.

Jeffers, Robinson. *The Selected Poetry of Robinson Jeffers,* ed. Tim Hunt. Stanford, CA: Stanford University Press, 2001.

Johnson, Robert. *Owning Your Own Shadow: Understanding the Dark Side of the Psyche.* San Francisco: HarperCollins, 1991.

Jung, Carl. *Man and His Symbols.* New York: Doubleday, 1964.

———————. *Memories, Dreams, Reflections,* ed. Aniela Jaffe. New York: Random House, 1989.

Kammen, Carole, and Jodi Gold. *Call to Connection: Bringing Sacred Tribal Values Into Modern Life.* Salt Lake City, UT: Commune-A-Key Publishing, 1998.

Kane, Dency, Lauri Brunton, and Erin Fournier. *Sanctuary: Gardening for the Soul.* New York: Friedman/Fairfax Publishers, 1999.

Karasu, T. Byram. *The Art of Serenity.* New York: Simon & Schuster, 2003

Kedar, Karyn D. *God Whispers: Stories of the Soul, Lessons of the Heart.* Woodstock, VT: Jewish Lights Publishing, 2000.

Kidd, Sue Monk. *When the Heart Waits: Spiritual Direction for Life's Sacred Questions.* Reprint, San Francisco: HarperSanFrancisco, 1992.

Kornfield, Jack. *The Art of Forgiveness, Lovingkindness, and Peace.* New York: Bantam Books, 2002.

Kurtz, Ernest, and Katherine Ketcham. *The Spirituality of Imperfection: Storytelling and the Search for Meaning.* New York: Bantam, 1992.

Kushner, Harold S. *Living a Life That Matters.* New York: Random House, 2002.

Lawrence, D. H. *Studies in Classic American Literature.* New York: Penguin, 1964.

Lemle, Mickey, producer and director. *Hasten Slowly: The Journey of Sir Laurens van der Post* (VHS). New York: Lemle Pictures, Inc., 1996.

Leonard, Linda Schierse. *The Call to Create: Celebrating Acts of Imagination.* New York: Harmony Books, 2000.

Levine, Stephen. *A Year to Live: How to Live This Year As If It Were Your Last.* New York: Bell Tower, 1997.

Luke, Helen M. *Old Age: Journey Into Simplicity.* New York: Parabola Books, 1987.

Luskin, Fred. *Forgive for Good: A Proven Prescription for Health and Happiness.* San Francisco: HarperSanFrancisco, 2001.

Lustbader, Wendy. *What's Worth Knowing.* New York: Jeremy P. Tarcher/Putnam, 2001.

Mabey, Juliet. *God's Big Book of Virtues.* Boston: Oneworld, 1998.

MacKenna, Stephen, ed. *The Enneads.* London: Faber & Faber, 1956.

Mahdi, Louise Carus, Nancy Geyer Christopher, and Michael Meade, eds. *Crossroads: The Quest for Contemporary Rites of Passage.* Chicago: Open Court, 1996.

Maxwell, William, ed. *The Letters of Sylvia Townsend Warner.* New York: Norton & Co., 1982.

Maybury-Lewis, David. *Millennium: Tribal Wisdom and the Modern World.* New York: Viking, 1992.

McLeish, John A.B. *The Ulyssean Adult: Creativity in the Middle and Later Years.* Toronto: McGraw-Hill Ryerson Limited, 1976.

Mead, Margaret. *Culture and Commitment.* New York: Anchor Press/Doubleday, 1978.

Meier, C. A. *A Testament to the Wilderness: Ten Essays on an Address.* Santa Monica, CA: The Lapis Press, 1985.

Merton, Thomas, ed. *The Wisdom of the Desert.* New York: New Directions, 1960.

_____. *A Grateful Heart,* ed. M. J. Ryan. Berkeley, CA: Conari Press, 1994.

Miller, Betty. *Robert Browning, A Portrait.* New York: Scribner, 1953.

Mills, Billy, and Nicholas Sparks. *Wokini: A Lakota Journey to Happiness and Self-Understanding.* New York: Orion Books, 1990.

Moody, Harry R., and David Carroll. *The Five Stages of the Soul: Charting the Spiritual Passages That Shape Our Lives.* New York: Anchor Books, 1997.

Moore, Thomas. *Care of the Soul.* New York: HarperCollins, 1992.

_____. *The Soul's Religion: Cultivating a Profoundly Spiritual Way of Life.* New York: HarpersCollins Publishers, 2002.

Morgan, Richard Lyon. *Fire in the Soul: A Prayer Book for the Later Years.* Nashville, TN: Upper Room Books, 2001.

Muller, Wayne. *Learning to Pray: How We Find Heaven on Earth.* New York: Bantam Books, 2003.

Murdock, Maureen. *Unreliable Truth: On Memoir and Memory.* New York: Seal Press, 2003.

Needleman, Jacob. *A Little Book on Love.* New York: Dell Publishing, 1996.

Nouwen, Henri J.M. *Reaching Out: The Three Movements of the Spiritual Life.* New York: Image Books, Doubleday, 1986.

Nowell-Smith, Simon. *Browning Poetry and Prose.* Boston: Harvard University Press, 1951.

O'Donohue, John. *Eternal Echoes: Exploring Our Yearnings to Belong.* New York: HarperCollins, 1999.

_____. *Conamara Blues.* New York: HarperCollins, 2001.

_____. *Beauty: The Invisible Embrace.* New York: HarperCollins, 2004

Oman, Maggie, ed. *Prayers for Healing: 365 Blessings, Poems, and Meditations From Around the World.* Berkeley, CA: Conari Press, 1997.

O'Neal, David, ed. *Meister Eckhart, From Whom God Hid Nothing*. Boston and London: Shambhala Publications, 1996.

Ouspensky, P. D. *In Search of the Miraculous: Definitive Exploration of G. I. Gurdjieff's Mystical Thought and Universal View*. New York: Harcourt Books, 2001.

Parabola: Myth, Tradition, and the Search for Meaning. Mask and Metaphor: Role, Imagery, Disguise, vol. 6:3 (Summer 1981).

Parabola: Myth, Tradition, and the Search for Meaning. Miracles, vol. 22:4 (Winter 1997).

Parabola: Myth, Tradition, and the Search for Meaning. Fear, vol. 23:3 (Fall 1998).

Parabola: Myth, Tradition, and the Search for Meaning. Threshold, vol. 25:1 (Spring 2000).

Patten, Christine Taylor. *Miss O'Keeffe*. Albuquerque, NM: University of New Mexico Press, 1998.

Perls, T. T., M. Silver, and J. F. Lauerman. *Living to 100: Lessons in Living to Your Maximum Potential at Any Age*. New York: Basic Books, 1999.

Peterson, Peter G. *Gray Dawn: How the Coming Age Wave Will Transform America — and the World*. New York: Times Books, 1999.

Piercy, Marge. *The Moon Is Always Female*. New York: Alfred A. Knopf, a division of Random House,1980

Pierrakos, Eva. *The Pathwork of Self-Transformation*. New York: Bantam, 1990.

Pipher, Mary. *Another Country: Navigating the Emotional Terrain of Our Elders*. New York: Riverhead Books, 1999.

Powell, Douglas H. *The Nine Myths of Aging: Maximizing the Quality of Later Life*. New York: W.H. Freeman and Company, 1998.

Progoff, Ira, *At a Journal Workshop: Writing to Access the Power of the Unconscious and Evoke Creative Ability*. New York: Jeremy P. Tarcher/Putnam, 1975, 1992.

Radlowski, Roger J., and John S. Kirran. *The Spirit of Poland*. Minneapolis, Winston Press, 1980.

Remen, Rachel Naomi. *My Grandfather's Blessings: Stories of Strength, Refuge, and Belonging*. New York: Putnam Publishing Group, 2000.

Richards, M. C. *Centering: In Pottery, Poetry, and Person.* Middletown, CT: Wesleyan University Press, 1964.

Richo, David. *Shadow Dance: Liberating the Power and Creativity of Your Dark Side.* Boston: Shambhala Publications, 1999.

Rifkin, Ira, ed. *Spiritual Innovators: Seventy-Five Extraordinary People Who Changed the World in the Past Century.* Woodstock, VT: Skylight Paths Publishing, 2002.

Roberts, Elizabeth, and Elias Amidon, eds. *Life Prayers From Around the World.* San Francisco: HarperSanFrancisco, 1996.

_____. *Prayers for a Thousand Years.* San Francisco: HarperSanFrancisco, 1999.

Robinson, Paschal, trans. *The Writings of St. Francis of Assisi.* Philadelphia: Dolphin Press, 1906.

Robinson, Roxana. *Georgia O'Keeffe: A Life.* Dartmouth, NH: University Press of New England, 1999.

Rowe, John, and Robert L. Kahn. *Successful Aging.* New York: Dell Publishing, 1998.

Rupp, Joyce. *Dear Heart, Come Home: The Path of Midlife Spirituality.* New York: The Crossroad Publishing Company, 2001.

Russack, Neil. *Animal Guides: In Life, Myth, and Dreams.* Toronto: Inner City Books, 2002.

Ryan, M. J., ed., *A Grateful Heart.* Berkeley, CA: Conari Press, 1994.

_____. *The Power of Patience: How to Slow the Rush and Enjoy More Happiness, Success, and Peace of Mind Every Day.* New York: Broadway Books, a division of Random House, 2003.

Sarton, May. *At Seventy.* New York: W.W. Norton, 1984

Schachter-Shalomi, Zalman, and Ronald S. Miller. *From Age-ing to Sage-ing: A Profound New Vision of Growing Older.* New York: Warner Books, 1995.

Schaub, R.N., Bonney Gulino, and Richard Schaub. *Dante's Path: A Practical Approach to Achieving Inner Wisdom.* New York: Gotham Books, 2003.

Schechter, Howard. *Jupiter's Rings: Balance From the Inside Out.* Ashland, OR: White Cloud Press, 2002.

Schutz, Will. *The Truth Option: A Practical Technology for Human Affairs.* Berkeley, CA: Ten Speed Press, 1984.

Seuss, Dr. (Theodor Geisel), and A. S. Geisel. *You're Only Old Once!* New York: Random House, 1986.

Sewell, Marilyn, ed. *Cries of the Spirit: A Celebration of Women's Spirituality.* Boston: Beacon Press, 1991.

Smith, Huston. *Why Religion Matters: The Fate of the Human Spirit in an Age of Disbelief.* New York: HarperCollins, 2001.

Somé, Sobonfu E. *Falling Out of Grace: Meditations on Loss, Healing, and Wisdom.* El Sobrante, CA: North Bay Books, 2003.

Straub, Gail. *The Rhythm of Compassion: Caring for Self-Connecting With Society.* Boston: Tuttle Publishing, 2000.

Stryk, Lucien, and Takashi Ikemoto, trans. *Zen Poems of China and Japan: The Crane's Bill.* New York: Grove Press, 1973.

Suzuki, David, and Peter Knudtson. *Wisdom of the Elders: Sacred Native Stories of Nature.* New York: Bantam Books, 1992.

Teasdale, Wayne. *The Mystic Heart: Discovering a Universal Spirituality in the World's Religions.* Novato, CA: New World Library, 1999, 2001.

Teilhard de Chardin, Pierre. *The Divine Milieu.* New York: Harper & Row, 1960.

_____. *Pierre Teilhard de Chardin: Writings.* New York: Orbis Books, publishing arm of Maryknoll Fathers & Brothers, 1999.

Tolstoy, Leo. *A Confession and Other Religious Writings.* New York: Penguin Classics, 1988.

Underhill, Evelyn. *Mysticism: The Nature and Development of Spiritual Consciousness.* Oneworld Publication, 1993.

Upanishads, trans. Juan Mascaro (Classic Series). New York: Viking Penguin, 1965.

van Swaaij, Louise, and Jean Klare. *The Atlas of Experience.* New York: Bloomsbury Publishing, 2000.

Vass-Lehman, Molly, Paula W. Jamison (ed.), Thomas Holmes, and Gayl Walker. *Seeds of Awakening: Cultivating and Sustaining the Inner Life.* Kalamazoo: New Issues Press, Western Michigan University, 2001.

Vaughan, Frances. *Shadows of the Sacred: Seeing Through Spiritual Illusions.* Wheaton, IL: The Theosophical Publishing House, 1995.

von Franz, Marie-Louise. *On Dreams and Death: A Jungian Interpretation,* trans. Emmanuel Xipolitas Kennedy and Vernon Brooks. Boston: Shambhala., 1986.

Wall, Steve. *Wisdom's Daughters: Conversations With Women Elders of Native America.* New York: HarperCollins Publishers, 1993.

Walsh, Roger. *Essential Spirituality: The Seven Central Practices to Awaken Heart and Mind.* New York: John Wiley & Sons, Inc., 1999.

Whitman, Walt. *Leaves of Grass.* New York: Bantam, 1983.

Wiesenthal, Simon. *The Sunflower: On the Possibilities and Limits of Forgiveness* (rev. and expanded ed.). New York: Schocken Books, 1976, 1997, 1998.

Wilder, Thorton. *The Bridge of San Luis Rey.* Cutchogue, NY: Buccaneer Books, 1991.

Wilhelm, Richard, trans. *The Secret of the Golden Flower: A Chinese Book of Life.* Orlando, FL: Harcourt, Brace & Co., 1962.

Yolen, Jane. *Gray Heroes: Elder Tales From Around the World.* New York: Penguin Putnam, 1999.

Zubko, Andy. *Treasury of Spiritual Wisdom: A Collection of 10,000 Inspirational Quotations.* San Diego, CA: Blue Dove Press, 1998.

www.artquotes.net. Jan. 2004.

www.bible.com. Aug. 2003.

www.nitaleland.com/quotations. Sept. 2003.

www.quoteworld.org. Aug. 2003.

www.unityofflagstaff.org/prayers/Navajo. Oct. 2004.

about the
Author

Angeles Arrien, PhD (1940 – 2014) received her master's degree from the University of California at Berkeley, and her doctorate from the California Institute for Integral Studies. Dr. Arrien's teachings bridge the disciplines of anthropology, psychology, and comparative religion, while focusing on universal beliefs shared by humanity. She lectured and led workshops internationally on cultural anthropology and transpersonal psychology at colleges, corporate settings, and personal growth facilities. Her books include *The Four-Fold Way*, *The Second Half of Life*, and *Living in Gratitude*, and her audio-learning programs include *Gratitude*, *Gathering Medicine*, and more.

about
Sounds True

Sounds True was founded in 1985 with a clear vision: to disseminate spiritual wisdom. Located in Boulder, Colorado, Sounds True publishes teaching programs that are designed to educate, uplift, and inspire. We work with many of the leading spiritual teachers, thinkers, healers, and visionary artists of our time.

To receive a free catalog of tools and teachings for personal and spiritual transformation, please visit www.soundstrue.com, call toll-free 800-333-9185, or write to us at the address below.

The Sounds True Catalog
PO Box 8010
Boulder CO 80306